OUTSMARTING

THE SOCIOPATH

NEXT DOOR

HOW TO PROTECT YOURSELF AGAINST

A RUTHLESS MANIPULATOR

Martha Stout, Ph.D.

HARMONY

BOOKS

Library of Congress Cataloging-in-Publication Data
Names: Stout, Martha, 1953- author. Title: Outsmarting the sociopath
next door : how to protect yourself against a ruthless manipulator /
Martha Stout, Ph.D. / Description: New York, NY : Harmony Books,
[2020] | Includes bibliographical references and index. / Identifiers:
LCCN 2019024151 | ISBN 9780307589071 (hardback) / ISBN
9780307589088 (trade paperback) / ISBN 9780307589095 (ebook)
Subjects: LCSH: Manipulative behavior—Prevention. / Psychopaths. /
Control (Psychology) Classification: LCC BF632.5 .S76 2020 / DDC
155.2/5—dc23. LC record available at https://lccn.loc.gov/2019024151.

ISBN 978-0-307-58907-1
Ebook ISBN 978-0-307-58909-5
International Edition ISBN 978-0-593-13819-9

Printed in the United States of America

Book design by Meighan Cavanaugh
Jacket design by Carlos Beltrán
Jacket photograph by Holger Winkler/Getty

10 9 8 7 6 5 4 3 2 1

First Edition

For my mother,

Martha Eva Deaton Stout,

1923–2018

Beautiful, more brilliant than she realized, and above all,

the kindest and most loving person I have ever known

Each one of us must take responsibility for our own lives, and above all, show respect and love for living things around us, especially each other.

—JANE GOODALL, *Reason for Hope*

CONTENTS

DUELING WITH THE DEVIL

D ressed in a paint-stained shirt and frayed jeans and intent on cleaning the underside of a deck, I was certainly not looking the part of a professional psychologist one spring afternoon when a shiny new SUV, bearing two young children and their well-dressed mother, appeared in my driveway. The woman was wearing neatly applied makeup; still, she looked as if she had been crying for days, and my heart went out to her. Obviously relieved to have found me, despite my torn jeans and my initial astonishment, she said she had traveled two hours to get to the town she could only speculate was mine. She told me that she was involved in a "custody battle from hell" with someone who was frighteningly cold-blooded, and that she feared for the well-being of her daughter and son. "To save my children," she said, "I've got to duel with the devil. And I don't know how."

She was certain that her ex-husband did not really want to be a father, and that he was suing for custody only to keep her "under his thumb," which, given her love and concern for the children, he was accomplishing quite handily. I explained the power of presenting a serene (rather than panicky) demeanor whenever she encountered her ex-husband—to thwart his desire for visible evidence that he was controlling her emotions—and provided her with some suggestions to help her speak productively with her lawyer. When she left, I was glad to see that, replacing the hopelessness, there was a glimmer of resolve in her eyes.

As a psychologist, I had studied sociopathy and treated clinically traumatized victims for more than twenty-five years, and still I did not fully appreciate the overwhelming prevalence of sociopathic victimization until I began to write about it. Since my book *The Sociopath Next Door* was published, in 2005, I have been flooded with phone calls and letters from readers who have felt compelled to tell me of their own encounters with people who appear to have no conscience. So motivated have these readers been to tell me their stories that some have managed to acquire my unlisted home phone number or have waited outside my office door in Boston, hoping to catch me coming or going. But this was the first time someone had appeared at my house.

I decided to establish a website with a dedicated email address, so my readers could relate their experiences without having to embark on such desperate searches. As soon as I did, I began to receive a seemingly endless torrent of messages from all over the world. Most of the people who contacted me (and who continue to do so, daily) are dealing with a possible sociopath who is simply not avoidable: the opposing party in a custody battle, a boss or a coworker in a job too valuable to leave, an adult in their family, or, in perhaps the most excruciating situation of all, one of their own children.

The readers who seek me out are from both genders and many different walks of life, but they have certain experiences in common. They have all felt alone and more than a little crazy: each has believed him- or herself to be the only person ever fooled and manipulated by a human being who turned out to possess an alien mind. They have survived a reality-shattering relationship with at least one person incapable of guilt, remorse, or even concern. And, until they read *The Sociopath Next Door,* all of these survivors had assumed that no one would believe their strange story. My book had given them the concepts and the words to describe their experiences. Now they were searching for tools to protect themselves and their loved ones. It is for them, and for all people who find themselves in unavoidable struggles with the conscienceless, that I have written this book on how to prevail against a sociopath.

Nearly all the letters I have received over the years fall naturally into a few categories, and, in media appearances and private conversations since 2005, I have been asked countless questions on these same crucial topics. In this book, I will discuss all of them: the grim reality of sociopathic children and how to deal with them; specific methods you can use to overcome a sociopath who has targeted you at work; what to do when, terrifyingly, your opponent in a child custody struggle is a sociopath; assaultive sociopaths (including cyberassault); and the differences between a sociopath and a narcissist. The book includes a chapter on sociopathy in our corporations and governments also, and thoughts on the nature of good.

Most conscienceless people, seeking to blend in with the rest of society (and not wanting to be caught or imprisoned), commit "invisible" moral and interpersonal crimes. Contrary to popular misconceptions, sociopaths who turn to lethal violence are a small minority. They are far more likely to be destructive liars and manipulators who play brutal psychological, financial, and political games with our lives. They comprise the single largest subgroup of domestic abusers: people who attempt to enhance their sense of power and control by beating up on spouses, children, and the elderly in the privacy of their homes. This is one of the reasons we find them so difficult to identify. But when sociopaths do murder, the results disturb us deeply. I'll discuss the pattern seen in murderous sociopathic behavior, and how this form of aggression is motivated differently from non-sociopathic violence.

Psychologists are loath to recommend avoidance as the solution to a problem, but where sociopathy is concerned, avoidance is actually the optimal course. Whether violent or not, sociopaths live outside of the social contract that binds the rest of us, are uniquely destructive, and will never be able to engage in authentic personal or work relationships with anyone. Their sole preoccupation is to have power over other people, and the most advisable and least dangerous course of action is to avoid such people altogether. However, steering clear of the sociopath is not always possible.

In this book, I will provide you with tools for dealing with the sociopath you simply cannot avoid. You will read stories inspired by the many, many letters I was sent, accounts from people who watched in shock as the scaffolding of accepted human reality fell from beneath them, and who bravely tried to rescue themselves and the people they loved in a world that no longer made sense. They were forced to learn that sociopaths are more than just abstractions in a fleeting newscast or the subject of a shocking documentary; they are human beings who look like everyone else—so well camouflaged that their true nature may have gone unrecognized for years or even decades.

While I've changed all names and any identifying details in these stories, you'll find examples of individuals who have triumphed, men and women who have dealt successfully with people who appeared to have no conscience—but also sad and even frightening stories in which the ruthless seem to win in the end. Whether they conclude in success or in travesty, all of the stories illustrate the ways in which our traditional ideas about evil have blinded us to its true nature. Evil behavior emanates from an emotional hole, and being unaware of this has severely limited our ability to deal with ruthlessness in our day-to-day lives and in our society. The real world–based accounts in this book affirm that a new, rational understanding of the leading source of human evil—*the characterological and neuropsychological absence of conscience*—could give us a crucial advantage as we deal with sociopathic people in our lives, and as we face the human-mediated problems of our age. I believe that, for our personal safety and, indeed, for the well-being of the planet we live on, we must abandon our mistaken beliefs—our "sociopathy blindness"—and take a useful stance grounded in knowledge and competence.

We must learn that, despite their trademark lack of emotion, sociopaths are "emotion-eaters." They have an intense desire to witness their control over us by inciting our confusion, anger, and fear. They feed off the negative emotions of others. Knowing when and how *not* to display emotion—how to remain calm in the presence of a sociopath rather than feeding him with our immediate feelings—is a vital skill. He is playing a terrible game with you, but I will show you how to change the rules of the game.

In *The Sociopath Next Door*, I coined the first psychological definition of "conscience." Contrary to earlier ideas, it is not a thought process or a set of internalized rules; rather, true conscience is a compelling emotion based in an attachment to another living creature (often but not always a human being), or to a group of human beings, or even, in some instances, to humanity as a whole. I established that conscience does not exist without the neuropsychological capacity to form genuine emotional bonds with others, and I discussed the characteristics and causes of sociopathy—the *absence* of emotional attachments and conscience—and the deep wounds the sociopath can inflict, with utter emotional impunity.

In the present book, I hope to provide an even greater understanding of the thoughts and behaviors that result from having a hole in the psyche where the emotion of conscience should be. I will offer real-world illustrations of the overarching pattern of gamesmanship in all sociopathic behavior, a picture that reveals itself before our eyes, over and over again, though most of us have not been taught how to "see" it. In a world of pedophile priests and CEOs who would sell their souls—and our planet—for more money, of manipulative custody battles that are in anything but the best interest of the child, and phony experts who spend their days casually scamming the elderly and the poor, we need to recognize this modus operandi.

What chance does an honest person have against a clever sociopath, a disguised adversary whose special powers are duplicity and absolute shamelessness? How does someone with normal emotional reactions to the suffering of others defeat an enemy who can guiltlessly do anything at all, no matter how destructive or cruel? How can a sincere and forthright person convince others of a sociopath's true nature when this calculating pretender fools and manipulates even extremely intelligent people, sometimes just for the thrill of making them jump?

My goal in this book is to provide clear and practical answers to these questions and to deal head-on with the fearful self-doubts that arise when people of conscience must oppose ruthless manipulators. To the woman who showed up on my doorstep and so many others, I offer answers that are optimistic and emboldening. As an honest, caring person, you have far more power than you know. Seeing the pattern, understanding the true nature of sociopathy, and, most crucially, *possessing effective methods to thwart the sociopath's agenda* will allow you to identify sociopathy confidently and respond with wise and powerful action when life absolutely requires you to take a stand.

ONE

A HOLE IN THE PSYCHE

Understanding Sociopathy

"The hardest thing to hide is something that is not there."

—ERIC HOFFER

In order to explain why the strategies I offer will succeed, I must first pose a seemingly paradoxical challenge to one of your most basic beliefs about how the world works. Imagine there is no such thing as evil. If you are a religious person, imagine there is no Satan, no Prince of Darkness, no deuce, no demon—no devil by any name. If you are not religious, ponder how you would feel, and how many of your ideas about life would change, after discovering that evil simply does not exist as an entity in our world. Yet more startling, suppose you were to learn that evil has *never* existed, not as a thing or as a wily supernatural being, not as a mysterious force or an unseen spirit, not even as some especially shameful part of ordinary human nature. I ask you to take this idea to the limit, to imagine that evil is no more than an ancient myth, like Norse trolls, or Sasquatch, or volcano gods who require the sacrifice of village maidens.

"What would be the point?" you might respond. "To think this way, we'd have to ignore too much about life as it is." Our world is full of evildoing and people who seem terrifyingly good at it. Maybe evil is not a force, or a thing, or a being with horns—maybe evil does not exist as a noun, so to speak—but the word *evil* certainly works well as a universally understood adjective: there are "evil" events, "evil" schemes, "evil" behaviors. And human beings seem to have a shared understanding of what kinds of events, schemes, and behaviors these are. So, if evil does not exist, what on earth are we talking about when we use the word?

I ask you to understand that there is no such thing as evil because, psychologically speaking, there is not. Wickedness is not an invasive spirit or thing, nor is it some shadowy part of the primal human brain. It is the opposite: rather than an entity that we could observe or at least feel, evil is an absence. Instead of *something,* it is a hollowness where something *should have been.*

True evil is an empty hole, nothing more—and nothing less. The neurology behind this "hole" will be described in the next chapter. For now, let's continue our discussion of how it reveals itself.

We consider some "evil" acts to be worse than others: serial murder and ethnic genocide are considered more heinous than, say, stealing an employee's pension. Understandably, we make these judgments based on the magnitude of the effects—on how lethal an act was—and how many people were affected. Invading someone's home and torturing a family for sport is seen as evil;

murdering millions of innocent people is regarded as profoundly so. But all genuinely evil behaviors, from vast and unspeakable crimes against humanity to tormenting one's spouse or embezzling someone's savings, are enabled by the same hole in the psyche.

We can begin to understand the nature of this hole—this unfathomed empty space that begins in neurological underdevelopment—by considering the following two versions of a story about a simple car accident. In the first telling of the tale, both people involved have ordinary brains and are psychologically whole. In the second version, one of the two individuals has something missing from his brain, literally, though most of his friends and family members would be shocked to learn this.

In the first account of this fictitious car accident, Tom and Jack (both with normal brains) are driving down a nearly empty road on a rainy night, going in opposite directions. Forgetting for a few moments that there could be oncoming traffic, Tom has drifted to the middle of the road and is driving on the yellow line. When Jack comes along, traveling the other way, the two cars come within a hair's breadth of a high-speed collision, and, to avoid the absentminded Tom, Jack is forced to drive his car off the road into a rain-flooded ditch.

Miraculously, neither of them is seriously hurt. They get out of their cars and approach each other on the dark, empty road. Tom is shaken and embarrassed. Jack is shaken, too, and enraged; his expensive car is brand-new, and he has painstakingly polished it for a rendezvous with an attractive woman he had wanted very much to impress tonight.

He yells at Tom, "What the holy hell were you doing, you idiot?"

Tom is a family man, just trying to get home. Recognizing a rhetorical question when he hears one, he apologizes diplomatically, several times, and then suggests that, if they work together, maybe they could get Jack's car out of the ditch. With some difficulty, they manage to do so, but in the process both men ruin their clothing with mud and wet grass.

Now Jack is far beyond enraged. Observing the condition of his clothes and the brown-green muck dripping from his formerly pristine car, he would like nothing better than to take some revenge. His thoughts flash on the dark humor of the .22 Beretta in his car. He had recently purchased it for protection, after hearing about some carjackings near this very road. Right now, the road is empty and dark. All he would have to do is open his car door, grab the pistol out of the gun safe, and *bang!*—no more idiot.

But, as you may have guessed, Jack does not shoot Tom. He is so infuriated that he might like to kill him, but he does not. More important, he *cannot,* because to shoot a stranger point-blank, to murder someone who has never so much as threatened him, is not a psychological option for him. Jack's brain, being normal, contains sensitive neurological structures that allow him to feel linked with his fellow human beings. Because of this strong inborn sense of connection—an attribute that includes an ability to love his family and friends, and to feel empathy for people in general—Jack's psyche contains the forceful intervening emotion we refer to as *conscience.* And right now, his conscience is fairly screaming at him, *Thou shalt not kill. Taking someone's life is evil.*

He begins to feel queasy, disturbed that he even thought about the gun, so he swallows his rage, writes down Tom's phone number, and gets back into his car. Scowling and muttering epithets, he drives away, covered with mud and terribly angry—but not a murderer.

Now we turn to the second version of the story. Tom #2, like Tom #1, is an everyday sort of fellow with a typically constructed brain that permits him to be psychologically normal. But Jack #2 is different from Jack #1. The second Jack's brain, being absent of any emotional connection to his fellow humans, has left him with a seriously abnormal psyche. Still, his aberrations usually go unidentified and even unnoticed by other people, except when circumstances—such as our fictitious car accident—cause them to loom especially large.

Jack #2 and Tom #2 are once again driving in opposite directions on a dark, empty road. As before, Tom has absentmindedly drifted to the center line. When Jack comes along, he and Tom avoid a head-on collision by the skin of their teeth, and Jack is forced to drive his expensive new car completely off the road and into a muddy ditch. Both men escape serious injury, but Jack is enraged.

Believing that Tom nearly got him killed, and remembering the good-looking woman he is supposed to be meeting later, Jack #2 screams the same thing the first Jack did: "What the holy hell were you doing, you idiot?"

Tom apologizes deferentially, just as before, and suggests they try to get Jack's car out of the ditch. They work together and get the car back up to the road, but in so doing, saturate their clothing with gunk.

Jack's rage is now over the top. He wants to kill Tom; he imagines how gratifying it would be to grab his unmarked .22 from the car and shoot the guy in the head. Checking out the road in both directions, he sees no other vehicles. Visibility has been bad all evening, and now a heavy fog is coming in. He could kill this guy, get back in his car, and simply keep driving. Odds are he would get away with it. When the body was finally discovered, people would think the murder involved a lovers' fight, or maybe a carjacking gone wrong.

He reaches through the car window, opens the glove box, and fingers the grip of the pistol lying inside. It feels good. His conscience does not speak to him because, unlike Jack #1, Jack #2 has only an empty space in his mind where human connection and conscience would normally be. Since he can experience none of the standard emotions of connection, this Jack feels nothing except (1) his wrath over the botched evening, and (2) his urge to kill Tom.

He takes the gun out of the car and aims it at a spot between Tom's eyebrows. In astonishment and terror, Tom lifts his arms as if to protect himself and starts to say, "Wait!" But before he can finish the word, Jack fires.

His face frozen in wide-eyed disbelief, Tom falls to the pavement, and his life's blood begins to form a dark, rain-splattered pool on the asphalt. Now Jack feels a rush. He gets into his fine new car and drives away, leaving the stranger for dead. Ten miles down the road, he is still smiling.

JACK'S SECRET CONDITION

Jack #2 was born with a subtle deficiency in his brain that resulted in a gaping hole in his emotional life. He is a sociopath, and, as with most sociopaths, his condition is all but invisible to other people. Indeed, the only person with an inkling of the truth has just been killed. While most altercations with sociopaths will not end in someone's death, it is important to realize that the only thing holding them back is not conscience but a desire to remain under the radar.

Though Jack does a good job of displaying counterfeit emotions when he needs to appear normal, for him there is only emptiness where genuine interpersonal feelings should be. Most people who know him would be amazed to discover that Jack is completely incapable of experiencing the warm emotions of relationships, including love. He can pretend convincingly, but is never an actual friend to anyone and cannot feel even a small amount of genuine concern for his fellow human beings. He cannot love or feel authentic concern for his family members, though he may claim to have these feelings. He has no real interest in bonding with a mate; if he marries, the union will be loveless, one-sided, and almost certainly short-term. If his spouse has any value to him, it will be because he views her as a possession, one he may feel *angry* to lose, but never genuinely sad. Should he become a father, he will not be able to love even his children.

It is often this last deficit that finally illuminates the true gravity and horror of the sociopathic condition. Since Jack #2 will be incapable of loving his own future children, how much empathy or even regard could one expect him to feel for an annoying stranger begging for his life by the side of the road, or for the children of that stranger? None at all.

The warm feelings that are part of normal human bonding (love of family and friends, caring, affection, gratitude) are the basis of what we call *conscience*; without them, conscience cannot be. Conscience is ever-present in the lives of people who are emotionally whole. Many of us feel some sting of its authority when we are even mildly selfish—when we, say, drink the last of the family's orange juice, or pocket the ten dollars we find between the sofa cushions, or deflate someone's mood with a thoughtless remark. In chilling contrast, Jack feels not even a small twinge of guilt when he robs a man of his life, and unseen children of their father. An empty hole in Jack's psyche turns unimaginably cruel acts into behavior that is natural and easy for him. Normal human nature did not enable Jack to do this; it would have railed against such an idea, and had Jack proceeded anyway, conscience would have clouded the rest of his life with feelings of shame. And neither did the devil make him do it. A particular psychological and neurological emptiness *allowed* him to do it, by making Jack incapable of human bonding in the first place.

In many different situations, not just along dark and dangerous highways, we count on the basics of human connection and conscience to moderate the behavior of other people, and, most of the time, our expectations are met. We assume that people will abide by the bottom-line proscription of *Thou shalt not kill.* We believe that nearly all adults will be reasonably gentle with young children. We rely on the idea that other people will honor their promises, especially when those promises are formalized as contracts. We count on bankers, brokers, and advisers not to steal from us. We trust friends and family not to use privileged, intimate information about us for their own gain. And our justice system depends on the notion that people will not lie after they have sworn before God not to do so. Surprisingly, even twenty-first-century society relies rather heavily on the honor system, and when we encounter an individual who simply is not bound by honor, conscience, or connection, we may find ourselves in big trouble. We can be thrown off balance and into jeopardy whether we meet that person on an isolated highway or in a boardroom, or a courtroom, or at home, in the vulnerable terrain of our personal relationships.

We are endlessly bewildered by the ruthless. When we hear of an especially abhorrent act, we call it "incomprehensible" and ask, *How could anyone do that? How can he stand to look at himself in the mirror?* And there is often a simple answer to our questions: The perpetrator is just fine around mirrors, because he does not possess the inner mechanism that would reflect unendurable guilt and shame back to him.

Few interactions with sociopaths are fatal, as was Tom's encounter with Jack #2, but contact is almost always destructive in one fashion or another. An association with a sociopath is perilous whether or not we realize the nature of the person we are dealing with—and at first, we usually do not. For example, the woman whom Jack is driving to meet in the story probably has no knowledge of his condition. Without a confluence of provocation and good opportunity, as there was with poor Tom on that dark and isolated road, Jack will not murder her.

Even a sociopath can curb his inclinations when discovery and punishment are extremely likely. Still, if she takes up with Jack, he almost certainly will harm her emotionally, financially, or in some other way less likely to interest the authorities. If she has money, or a usable social or professional connection, or anything else Jack is interested in, he will find a way to make it his. In general, he will try to control and manipulate her, often just for the fun of it. The more of her life she shares with him, the more severely her life will be damaged.

But if she is like most people who encounter sociopaths, she will doubt her personal value and her own sanity more readily than she will credit the simple but mind-boggling truth: Jack does not have a conscience.

THE SOCIOPATH DEFINED

The concept of sociopathy is anything but new. For at least two centuries, the condition of having no conscience has been described by observers of human behavior all over the world and called by various names, including *manie sans délire*, moral insanity, moral imbecility, psychopathic inferiority, psychopathy, and sociopathy. In my work, I use the term *sociopathy*, but there is no universally agreed-upon distinction between that designation and any of the others, including psychopathy. A popular idea is that a "psychopath" is violent and a "sociopath" is not, but this conception is inaccurate. The two terms are often used interchangeably, and both refer to a person who is devoid of conscience but who may or may not be prone to violence. A mental illness having the central characteristic of guiltlessness was the first personality disorder to be recognized by modern psychiatry. In 1812, University of Pennsylvania professor Benjamin Rush, known as the father of American psychiatry, wrote of individuals who appeared to be afflicted with what he called a "perversion of the moral faculties." In 1994, a "pervasive pattern of disregard for and violation of the rights of others," a condition similar to the one noted by Rush, was listed in the American Psychiatric Association's *Diagnostic and Statistical Manual of Mental Disorders IV* (*DSM-IV*)—the so-called bible of psychiatric disorders—by the more reserved name of "antisocial personality disorder."

According to a newer (2013) version of the manual (*DSM-5*), antisocial personality disorder is "characterized by a pervasive pattern of poor social conformity, deceitfulness, impulsivity, criminality, and lack of remorse" and is diagnosable when *three or more* of the following seven "pathological personality traits" are present:

1. **Manipulativeness:** Frequent use of subterfuge to influence or control others; use of seduction, charm, glibness, or ingratiation to achieve one's ends.
2. **Deceitfulness:** Dishonesty and fraudulence; misrepresentation of self; embellishment or fabrication when relating events.
3. **Callousness:** Lack of concern for feelings or problems of others; lack of guilt or remorse about the negative or harmful effects of one's actions on others; aggression; sadism.
4. **Hostility:** Persistent or frequent angry feelings; anger or

irritability in response to minor slights and insults; mean, nasty, or vengeful behavior.

5. **Irresponsibility:** Disregard for—and failure to honor—financial and other obligations or commitments; lack of respect for—and lack of follow-through on—agreements and promises.

6. **Impulsivity:** Acting on the spur of the moment in response to immediate stimuli; acting on a momentary basis without a plan or consideration of outcomes; difficulty establishing and following plans.

7. **Risk-taking:** Engagement in dangerous, risky, and potentially self-damaging activities, unnecessarily and without regard for consequences; boredom proneness and thoughtless initiation of activities to counter boredom; lack of concern for one's limitations and denial of the reality of personal danger.

The scientists who compile such diagnostic descriptions attempt to speak in terms of directly observable behaviors, rather than referring to internal states and emotions that would require the diagnostician to be a mind reader. Partly for this reason—and partly because notions that touch on the subject of morality are deemed to have no place in psychiatric nomenclature—the *DSM* never mentions the word *conscience*. Instead it refers, for example, to behavioral traits like *callousness* and *deceitfulness*, more observable characteristics than is conscience or its lack.

The behaviors of sociopathic deceitfulness (such as "dishonesty and fraudulence") are often facilitated by a glib and superficial charm that allows the sociopath to seduce other people, figuratively or literally—a kind of glow or charisma that, initially, can make the sociopath seem more interesting than the people around him. He or she is more spontaneous, more intense, more complex, more sexy, and more alluring than others. The sociopath's repertoire often includes isopraxism, a behavior that can be almost hypnotically engaging. *Isopraxism,* or reflexive mirroring, means duplicating another's body language, gestures, vocal tone, accent, word and metaphor choice, facial expression, and even breathing rate. It often occurs automatically between close friends, lovers, and people who are flirting. Usually unnoticed by either party, isopraxism tends to deepen a sense of trust and emotional closeness between two people in a healthy relationship.

Unfortunately, to beguile and maneuver a victim into a distinctly unhealthy liaison, the sociopath can consciously employ such trust-inducing behaviors—all the while supplying hyperbolic flattery and appearing to be fascinated by the victim's interests and concerns. In addition, the sociopath's charisma is sometimes accompanied by grandiose claims about himself that may captivate a "charmed" victim, but would probably sound odd or even laughable to a more objective listener ("Someday the world will realize how special I am," or "You know that after me, no other man will do").

Sociopaths have a much greater than normal need for excitement and stimulation, and this chronic need often results in their taking physical, financial, and socially shocking risks. ("Let's go to the beach during the hurricane" or "Why not invest all our money in this high-risk stock? I just know it's going to skyrocket!" or "Let's crash the boss's private wedding party. Don't you want to see the look on her face?") At the outset, such risks may seem adventurous and attractive to people whose lives have been more carefully led, and sociopaths readily charm others into attempting dangerous ventures with them. Afterward, they will refuse to acknowledge responsibility for any resulting damage to their conscience-bound companions.

In general, sociopaths are known for their pathological lying and conning, and their parasitic relationships with lovers and "friends." They are noted especially for their shallowness of emotion, the hollow and transient nature of any affectionate feelings they may claim to have, and a certain breathtaking callousness.

When challenged on his or her manipulative and callous behavior—and, in some cases, actual lawbreaking—the sociopath is adept at producing crocodile tears and playing the part of the wounded or vulnerable party. Indeed, as I discuss in *The Sociopath Next Door,* what I call the "pity play"—a behavior meant to exploit the normal person's tendency to feel sympathy and compassion—is often the only sign of sociopathy that is visible to the untrained eye. This usually happens after the sociopath has been discovered in some particularly egregious act and repeated claims of innocence have not been effective. Suddenly, the sociopath alleges that he or she is hurt, deeply depressed, dramatically remorseful, or physically ill. After the sociopath has been found out, a typical sequence of ploys is threefold: *protestations of innocence* ("Why would I do such a thing?"), followed by a *pity play* ("I've been feeling suicidal lately, and these accusations are going to push me over the edge!"), and finally, if neither denying the truth nor the pity play has succeeded in closing the issue, a stunning and seemingly incongruous display of rage that includes *threatening the accuser with harm* if she or he persists.

Though we may know all of the above "symptoms" of sociopathy, individual sociopaths often remain invisible to us. Because we cannot fathom the yawning chasm created by a missing conscience, we cannot "see," let alone understand, the true nature of the sociopath who may be standing in front of us or, even more dangerously, sleeping beside us. When we combine this lack of knowledge and understanding with the prevailing belief that, deep down somewhere, all human beings possess a conscience, we are nearly helpless in our dealings with people who are indeed conscienceless.

Making them still more difficult to recognize, most sociopaths simply do not look the part. With the exception of Charles Manson himself, they do not resemble Charles Manson. Their faces are not frightening or evil-looking; nor do sociopaths appear to be insane. They do not hide in dark corners, or speak in menacing voices, or foam at the mouth. Most sociopaths look and sound just like us. They vary widely in degree of education, intelligence, and talent, just as we do. They are to be found in minimum-wage jobs as well as in high-powered professional and political careers, and in all the many stations in between. They are welfare recipients and welfare policymakers, factory workers and factory owners, students, teachers, artists, doctors, lawyers, CEOs, and any other sort of person one might conceivably encounter in our society. They look like us, appear to have lives just like ours, and the great majority of them will never be chased by the police, tried in court, or thrown into prison.

Even more at odds with our popular notions of them, most of the "morally insane" are not murderers. Sociopaths control, manipulate, and destroy in countless ways, but most never escalate to the level of lethal violence. Bloodlust seems to be the ruling motivator for only a minority. For most, there is a decidedly more meaningful consideration: the conscienceless do not want to go to prison or to death row any more than normal people do, and homicide is much more likely to be discovered and seriously punished by the authorities than is, say, leading your lover into financial ruin, or quietly damaging your colleague's career, or carving permanent psychological scars into a vulnerable person's psyche. The guiltless have no internal mechanism to limit their behavior, but they are calculating by definition. When severe external consequences are likely, they can and often do control their actions via cold intellect, well enough to be invisible to the authorities.

When sociopaths do engage in physical aggression, usually the behavior occurs at home, hidden from public view. Sociopaths are the commonest perpetrators of recurrent sibling, elder, child, and spousal abuse, and this tendency is referred to in the *Diagnostic and Statistical Manual* in the description of *callousness,* which may include aggression and sadism. Domestic abuse is rarely prosecuted successfully, or prosecuted at all, so its consequences are less than forbidding from the sociopath's point of view.

One might easily imagine our prisons to be full of sociopaths, but this is not the case, either. To the contrary, getting caught and imprisoned for sociopathic acts is apparently more the exception than the rule. Those who conduct research on sociopathy (as well as individuals personally victimized by sociopaths) have discovered that sociopathic acts tend to involve crimes that fall under the radar of our current legal system. On average, only about 20 percent of prison inmates in the United States are sociopaths. To be sure, this 20 percent contains a disproportionate number of chronic offenders and accounts for more than half of the most serious crimes (extortion, armed robbery, kidnapping, the most brutal murders), including crimes against the state (treason, espionage, terrorism). Still, the sociopathic head count in prisons is only about two in ten. And even when formal laws of the land are broken, sociopaths are often able to deceive and manipulate judges and parole boards by putting on faux emotional displays and what University of British Columbia psychologist Stephen Porter describes as "Academy Award–winning performances." Dr. Porter's research indicates that sociopathic criminals move through the correctional system relatively quickly, and are granted early release more than twice as often as non-sociopathic criminals.

No one has a greater ability to deceive and manipulate than an intelligent sociopath who looks just like everyone else. I have asked countless former victims whether they had any early suspicions that they were being deceived, and nearly all have given the same answer. In the beginning, they saw someone who had a great deal of charm and an intense interest in what other people had to say, someone who was very complimentary. They saw no red flags. They were without a clue until they began to be victimized, and many remained so long after that. Professor Robert Hare of the University of British Columbia, who researched the prison statistics above, is the author of a psychological inventory called

Robert Hare's Psychopathy Checklist—Revised (the PCL-R), accepted as a standard diagnostic instrument for researchers and clinicians worldwide. Mincing no words, Hare writes of his subjects, "Everyone, including the experts, can be taken in, manipulated, conned, and left bewildered by them. A good psychopath can play a concerto on *anyone's* heartstrings. . . . Your best defense is to understand the nature of these human predators."

The veneer can be impenetrable, as their preoccupation with cat-and-mouse games, domination, and control is alien to us. The majority of human beings are quite decent. What we want primarily is to live our lives as happily and peacefully as possible, to take care of ourselves and our families, and to see our children grow up with the opportunity to do the same. Though we may have our selfish moments, overall we will labor hard and sacrifice much to preserve the well-being of the people we love, and to garner a sense of meaning from our work and activities. In our heart of hearts, we do not view life itself as a game. Life, for most of us, is a serious endeavor, and its best rewards are love and human connection. It can be disorienting—shocking, even—to discover that not all people can love, that not all human beings possess a conscience, and that a small conscienceless minority cause the lion's share of human suffering.

UNDERSTANDING THE CONSCIENCELESS

For most of our history, we have not understood—indeed, have resisted understanding—that the inability to develop a conscience is substantially inborn, changeless, and therefore unre-sponsive to appeals for compassion (or even rationality), the fear of God, moral concerns, and, to a large extent, our formal legal systems. We have been especially blind to the fact that psycho-logical denial—including our proclivity to view evil as an actual thing or a force outside of ourselves—allows the problem of so-ciopathy to flourish as it goes unseen.

We can advance our understanding of sociopathy by learning the answer to one very illuminating question: What is common among seemingly quite different conscienceless people? What does the bogus investor who swindles people out of their money have in common with the gruesome serial killer? And how do both the notorious con artist and the serial murderer resemble the uncounted non-newsworthy sociopaths who pass as normal in our society—or the office bully and the family tyrant? The answer, as you are beginning to find out, is an ice-cold, unfeeling emptiness. You will discover in the next chapter what the result-ing psychological anatomy looks like in all such individuals, re-gardless of the misleading differences among them.

An increased understanding of "evil" as a psychological and neurological *deficiency* may give you a sudden and perhaps jolt-ing paradigm shift. The inability to "see" sociopathy makes us vulnerable and afraid; but the opposite—knowing what socio-pathic emptiness looks like in the real world—can provide us with the vision to begin dealing with the ruthless in ways that are rational, humane, and effective, rather than panic-stricken, vengeful, and superstitious. In the next four chapters I will discuss four categories of sociopath: (1) when it's your child, (2) when it's someone you work with or have to deal with in a professional capacity, (3) when it's your opponent in a court battle for custody of your children, and (4) when it's someone who uses physical violence or bullies via the Internet. Following these categories is a chapter covering ten key guidelines for protecting yourself.

The most crucial and challenging rule when encountering sociopaths is the general principle espoused by Professor Robert Hare: *To defeat a sociopath, you must understand the nature of "human predators."* I hope the following pages give you a clear understanding of their nature so you can defend yourself against them, satisfy your need to "see" these people in a new way, and help you feel less crazy and alone.

In the next chapter, I address the issue most likely to create a fundamental change in your way of thinking about the meaning of evil, and in your ideas about bad people, good people, and perhaps our species in general. These first accounts are from loving parents struggling to deal with "empty" children—with sons and daughters who, contrary to our centuries-old conceptions of human nature, were born without the capacity to love.

What can parents do, ethically and humanely, when they are charged with raising a child who will never love anyone, not even them? To understand the enormity of this question, and to gain insight into the controversial subject of what sociopathy looks like in the very young, let us turn to the illustrative story of a boy named Silas on the morning after Superstorm Sandy in New York.

TWO

WHEN THE SOCIOPATH BELONGS TO YOU

Children Without Conscience

"I am having a very difficult time reconciling the beautiful child that I gave birth to with the monster that my eldest boy is."

—FROM A MOTHER IN TENNESSEE

"What kind of little girl gets a big kick out of watching her parents cry?"

—FROM A FATHER IN TORONTO

Eleven-year-old Silas thought his mother was an idiot for not taking them to a shelter before Superstorm Sandy reached Staten Island. On the other hand he was glad about it, because finally something was happening that was not completely boring. In his pitch-dark room, he had sat up in his cluttered twin bed all night, listening to the storm. Midland Beach was only a mile away, and the ocean and the wind had sounded like a giant freight train headed straight for the house. The walls had

shaken—he could actually feel them move—and with each cre-
scendo in the blast, Silas had said aloud, *"Excellent!"* Now, as the
storm began to pass, he thought about all the people out there
who had probably just died. That was unbelievably interesting.

When a faint suggestion of daylight strained through the
webs of duct tape his mother had put on the windows, he decided to get started. He figured he needed to leave really early,
before any of the remaining neighbors had the nerve to go outside, and before most of the rescue people got to the beach.
During the night, he had planned it all out. He would wear his
boots and his yellow jacket, which had a hood, and he would
bring along one of those large black trash bags that his mother
kept under the kitchen sink.

Now, going down the hall to the kitchen, he passed his mother's bedroom and saw that she was still in there with the door
closed. She would not try to keep him from leaving the house.
She had long since stopped arguing with him, let alone trying to
control him. Whatever Silas wanted to do, he did. He knew that
some part of her decision not to go to a shelter was her fear that
he would do something "shameful" in front of a lot of other
people. In fact, it was so easy to rattle her cage that it was hardly
even fun anymore. As for his father—he had left two years ago,
mainly because he could not deal with Silas.

Inside her bedroom, Silas's mother was awake. After hearing
footsteps in the hall, she opened her bedroom door, listened anx-
iously for a moment, and then slowly made her way to the
kitchen, sliding the fingertips of her right hand along the wall, as
if for balance. When she got there, Silas was pulling a plastic
trash bag out of a box.

"What are you doing?" she asked.

"None of your business," he replied.

He stuffed the bag into a jacket pocket and, without looking at her, opened the rain-slicked kitchen door and walked outside, into what she knew was a very dangerous dawn. She tried not to think this thought, but she could not help herself: How would she feel if he simply never came back? Honestly, she did not know, and the guilt of it squeezed her hard around the lungs. Ashamed and panic-stricken nearly always, she could not remember the last time she had been able to take a deep breath.

Silas went down the back stairs and slogged through standing water to reach the swampy front yard. It was obvious that the worst of the storm had moved on, but the metallic gray sky was still satisfyingly ominous. The first thing he noticed was that his house had escaped getting wrecked only by the skin of its teeth. Most of the houses across the street had been badly mutilated. One was missing its whole roof—decapitated, just like that. *"Excellent!"* he whispered to himself. He pulled up his hood and stepped out into the road, where walking through the flood was a little easier, and went to the cross street that led down toward the beach. At the very top of the intersection, where the road was not completely under water, there was a small blue-and-red crab on the asphalt, way out of place. He stopped and flipped the crab over with his boot, to see how it would react, but all it did was lie there, showing its drab underside and waving one of its claws. He pressed the crab's middle with his boot heel until the creature made a soft crunching noise, and then he continued down the road in the direction of the shore. When he got as far as the neighborhood playground, he saw a boat—an actual boat from the ocean—sitting there in front of the swings. This made him laugh out loud.

The area beyond the playground looked as if bombs had fallen. A lot of the houses were not there anymore, just the shells of their foundations. He did not even know where to start. *So, where would the dead people be?* As he tried to think this through, his eyes fell on the glimmer of something bright red inside the jagged gray foundation of the closest missing house. Avoiding the crop of snapped wires and cables that had sprung up everywhere, he climbed over a low wall of cinder blocks into the pathetic rectangle where people and all their stuff used to be. He was above his knees in water and God knows what else. There, wedged between two shards of floorboard, was the red object, which turned out to be a small stuffed-animal version of Clifford the Big Red Dog. He yanked it loose, examined the dripping-wet Clifford for a moment, and decided to put it into his trash bag—not money, obviously, but it was an okay thing.

A little farther in the direction of the ocean, there were a few houses that somehow had not been blown completely away from their foundations. One of these houses looked as if something had sliced it right down the middle, with the entire right half turned cockeyed. Where the house had been split open, there was a gap in the debris large enough for his eleven-year-old frame to squeeze through. Things inside the level half of the house were tossed around and wet, but the interior walls looked surprisingly intact. The people must have gotten out before the storm, because there were no dead bodies here. He looked around for anything that might appeal to him. On the floor of a bedroom, he found three shiny necklaces and a ring and dropped them into his bag, but nothing else in the house looked valuable, especially since all the electronics had been drenched. Going through the kitchen cabinets, he did come across a perfectly good package of Oreo cookies, and that went into the bag, too. In a kitchen drawer, he found a paper folder, more or less dry, filled with photos of a little boy's birthday party. He flipped through them and saw that the party had taken place in this very house. When they came back, the mom and dad would be happy to see that these pictures had survived, he reasoned, and then he grinned and tossed the photos into a large pool of murky water in the middle of the floor.

Thinking he might have time to try a better place before too many rescuers and cops showed up, he crawled back out of the sliced-in-half house. Not too far away, there was a bigger house that looked promising. Its entire wraparound porch had cracked off, so he had to walk across some planks that lay between the shifting porch and a giant open gash in the front wall of the house. It was sort of dicey, even for him, but he aced it. This time he checked the kitchen first, and immediately noticed that, through the storm, a flashlight and a box of candles had somehow managed to stay put on the kitchen table. Someone had stayed in this house last night, he was sure of it, and whoever it was had been expecting the power to go out. Maybe someone was still around.

"Hello! Is anybody here?" he called out.

No answer.

He needed to remember: When his ridiculous mother had decided to stay, what had she done to get ready for the storm? She had put duct tape on the windows, she had gotten out flashlights—and she had gone to the cellar and turned off the gas. He looked around the kitchen and saw an open door that led to some stairs, so he picked up the flashlight and started down them. Below him, something sparkled in the flashlight beam, and when he got to the bottom of the stairs, the floodwater in the cellar was up to his waist. He shone the flashlight around, and there it was—a body, floating facedown just below the surface of the water. It had white hair. *Probably some useless old man who should have gotten out of here before the storm came.* Silas sluiced through the water to get to the body and felt around underneath the guy for his pants pockets. The first pocket was empty, but sure enough, the second one had a wallet, which Silas extracted and held up to the flashlight. Inside, there were some stuck-together pictures, a credit card, and two $100 bills. *Score!*

He wanted to stay and stare at the drowned guy some more, but he knew he had to hurry. He gazed for one long last moment and then climbed back up to the kitchen, where he had left his big plastic bag. He put the sopping wallet inside with the other things and quickly looked around the rest of the house, but there was not much else to see, just a lot of books. As he was about to leave, he spotted a pile of CDs, and on top was one that said Yo-Yo Ma. He thought that was funny, so he dropped it into the bag with everything else and ceremoniously pulled the drawstring shut.

Outside, there were flashing lights now and some people wading around. He definitely did not want to get caught, and he was hungry and cold and soaking wet, so he tugged his hood lower over his face and headed for home. When he got there, his mother was again in her bedroom with the door shut. He went to his room and changed into dry clothes, fished the wallet out of the bag, and put the credit card and the two hundred dollars in his pocket. He pulled out the Oreos, took a dozen of them from the package, and set them in three neat stacks on the bed. Then he devoured them, twisting each one open and eating the icing first, as any kid would do.

Three days later, his mother sneaked into his room. If he had caught her, she would have said she was cleaning, but really she was trying to find the trash bag he had taken with him the morning after the storm. What had he been doing? She discovered the bag in his closet, hidden under a dirty shirt. Inside, she found a soggy Clifford the Big Red Dog, who was beginning to mildew, an open package of Oreos, a classical music CD, and some gold jewelry that looked real. And there was something else in the bag. She reached to the bottom and pulled out a curled and stiffened leather wallet. It held no money, just some ruined photos. After a moment, the probable source of the wallet occurred to her, and she flung it to the floor as if it were a poisonous spider. Trembling and short of breath, she sat down on Silas's small bed, covered her face with her hands, and wept for the child she had lost.

THE LOST CHILDREN

Silas, eleven years old, is death-defying, prone to cruelty and thievery, emotionally ice-cold, and unable to love. He is anything but an innocent child, and his story seems almost unreal. But the truth is that children like Silas exist in the real world.

The innocence of children is enormously important to adults. Children love us spontaneously, free of the harder edges we all eventually acquire during the course of our lives. They can remind us that, before the world taught us to conceal our grown-up selves under layers of anxious pretense, we too met our lives openly. Small children know almost no guile: they cry from frustration, pain, or genuine need and laugh only when they are truly delighted, which is often. Their direct experience of need, joy, and wonder—and, in a seeming miracle, their capacity to love without agenda—fulfills some of our most cherished ideas about what it means to be human.

Learning that innocence is not shared by all children can be existentially and even physically frightening. My first real-life lesson about non-innocent children was certainly frightening for me on the day when, as a young graduate student working at a psychology clinic, I was scheduled to do an intake evaluation on a twelve-year-old rapist. That day, when the time arrived for the one-to-one interview, my intellectual interest in the case was eclipsed by a sudden nameless anxiety and an uncomfortable wish not to meet the person who was waiting for me. Composing myself, I walked into the reception room, and what I saw there took me very much aback: he was just a twelve-year-old boy. If anything, he looked young for his age, a skinny kid pulling at the neck of the big sweater his mother had probably made him wear. His light brown hair fell into his face, and behind it his blue eyes looked bored, the way children's eyes often look in waiting rooms full of adults. He did not seem scary at all, and I believe I would have felt safer if he had.

I knew that, about a month before, this normal-looking boy

had ambushed his sister in her bedroom and raped her. His mother had kicked open the latched door to find her twelve-year-old son on top of her shrieking six-year-old daughter. Now, sitting in the waiting room, he was accompanied by the members of his family, who huddled close to each other as they waited: the boy, his exhausted-looking parents, and the six-year-old sister, who clung to her mother and appeared to want to climb into her lap.

When I escorted the boy into the private session room, he sat down in the chair across from mine and continued to look bored. His answers to my questions were brief, even for a kid his age.

I asked, "Do you know why you're here?"

"Yeah," he said.

Hoping he would say more, I asked, "Can you tell me why?"

He said, "Because of what I did."

"What did you do?"

"I guess I hurt my sister, or something."

"You hurt your sister? Do you feel bad about that?"

He looked around the small room for a moment. Then, finding nothing of interest, he looked back at me.

"Sure," he said.

The rest of my questions received similar answers, appropriate but unconvincing. I was able to learn almost nothing about him, apart from the facts already recorded in his chart. During the thirty minutes I sat with him, he showed no signs of violence or of any other overtly troubling behavior. On the other hand, strangely, he did not seem to feel guilty about his past behavior, or scared of his circumstances, or even embarrassed by my questions. Indeed, he showed no feelings at all. The only emotional reaction was my own, and it was a remarkable one: I was an adult, the authority in the situation, and he was diminutive and obedient—and yet I felt anxious being alone in a room with this child. By the time I told him he could return to the waiting room, my heart was beating fast and I felt a little dizzy.

He had been ordered into therapy by Child Protective Services and the Family Court. My part was simply to assign him to an appropriate therapist. I referred him to a psychologist who often worked with court-mandated patients, and after that one brief session, I never saw him again. Over the years, I have seen other children with equally disturbing histories, but, of them all, it is that particular boy I recall most vividly. Maybe this is because he was the first child rapist I had ever encountered. Or maybe it is the sad and exhausted faces of his parents, their eyes drained of laughter and vitality, that I cannot forget. I knew their troubles were just beginning. At that time, their son was a young boy, small enough to be taken to a therapist against his will. Later, he would become too old and too big to be forced into anything he did not want to do. I imagine that, perhaps not long after the day I met him, he began to do exactly as he pleased, whatever that happened to be, shattering his family and badly wounding other lives.

I had been stressed after only half an hour with him. What must have happened to his parents, the two people who could never escape him? Did they end up blaming themselves for his cold-bloodedness? And how did they deal with knowing that their destinies were irrevocably connected with his? How much fear and shame can parental love survive? What can it be like to be the mother or father of a child utterly unable to feel guilt?

The letters I receive from the parents of such children provide heartrending insight into what their lives are like. Each time I look at one of these letters, I experience the stomach-twisting concern that what I am reading is the panicked buildup to a state of complete despair—and I am always aware that each of these accounts represents only a single case from a great tide of anguished stories.

The following letter came to me from a desperate father:

I have a son who has been diagnosed as antisocial. He is 18 years old and the past five years have been living hell. After 6 schools that include a military school and summer schools, he graduated from high school. He has been extremely violent, heavily involved in drugs, and probably the nastiest person I have ever encountered. Nothing is ever his fault and he shows absolutely no remorse for anything. I have thrown him out of our house and he is living with my in-laws where he can successfully charm them into thinking he is just perfect.

While he was in school I handled the police, the expulsions from schools, the violent outbursts, the drug rehab centers, and everything else he has done. My problem is dealing with the flashbacks, the lack of understanding why this has happened, and the guilt that I let it go on for so long. I have tried counseling and they just don't seem to understand the magnitude of how bad it was.

I want to try to put a life back together for my wife, my younger son and myself. I also want to forgive [my older son] but right now I can't. My instincts tell me he will end up in jail and I know there is nothing I can do to stop it.

A similar account:

> *He was so smart, my son, but every ounce of his intelligence went to the dark side. I became aware of this around the time he began high school. Anyone he interacts with just suffers terribly. The person he called his best friend hanged himself. Every time he gets into a game with other kids, he ends up punching one or more of them, again and again. One day he put a hot iron on his six-year-old sister's neck. We had to take her to the hospital. It just doesn't stop.*

In these two brief stories, we can detect many of the common characteristics of guiltless children:

- Unremitting trouble at school
- Violence
- Involvement with drugs
- Hatefulness ("nastiness")
- Rejection of responsibility
- Remorselessness
- Convenient charm
- Manipulativeness
- Destruction of other people's lives
- Attacks on siblings

In addition, we can see some of the severe effects on parents:

- Exhaustion
- Trauma reactions (sometimes complete with flashbacks)

- Confusion
- Self-blame and guilt
- Sense of isolation, often even in counseling situations
- Disruption of the entire family
- Dread of the future

This mother's chilling story reveals another unimaginable situation often faced by the parents of guiltless children:

I took in my nephew when he was just a baby, after my sister begged me to. She told me it hadn't been planned and she wasn't ready to take care of a child. Most of all, she feared what her husband would be like as a father. My brother-in-law is a drunk who is prone to violence, but she can't seem to break away from him. Our son soon felt like ours, and he joined us and our daughter as we did our best to provide a loving home for him. But he was still a toddler when we realized that we had a chronic liar on our hands. He would try to make us pity him, pretending he'd been hurt or bullied by someone. Then he began stealing things from my daughter, always denying it when confronted. We had to monitor his behavior constantly. He always seemed to be on the verge of hitting someone, and I began to fear for my family's safety. We lock our bedroom doors to keep him from stealing our things, and now we lock them at night too, for fear he might try to hurt us as we sleep.

That the members of some families lock their bedroom doors at night because they fear physical harm from one of their children comes as shocking news to most people; however, it is not uncommon for guiltless children to be violent, even murderous, within their own homes. Typically, this kind of behavior is directed at the smallest and most vulnerable family members:

> *I didn't want to believe that my son, my own flesh and blood, could be a sociopath. No kind of parenting could stop him from being so destructive to my family. When Cindy was born five years after Robert, I almost regretted it. Not because I didn't love her to pieces, but because of what Robert did to her. Cindy was still in the crib when Robert began molesting her. We found inexplicable burns on her arms and bruises on her legs. We tried to be vigilant, but it was not enough.*
>
> *Then it happened. Cindy was only two, and walking was still a new milestone for her. We had put up a gate to block the entry to the basement so she couldn't fall down the stairs. I had let my guard down just for a few minutes so I could fold laundry in the bedroom. I thought Robert was playing outside. Then I heard something crashing, over and over, down the stairs. I rushed down and saw my daughter lying there at the bottom, her body crumpled and lifeless on the concrete basement floor. When I looked up, I saw Robert standing at the top of the stairs, showing no surprise or shock. He shrugged his shoulders and told me that Cindy must have figured out how to open the gate. We knew without a doubt that he had killed our beautiful baby.*

Too often, the parents of terrifying children such as Robert are not served well by the understated and confusing language of psychiatry. After Robert let his baby sister fall to her death, his mother began to refer to him as a sociopath, and her reasons for thinking of him this way are abundantly clear to anyone who knows her story. Technically, however, a seven-year-old would not be given this diagnosis within the current diagnostic system for mental illness. The American Psychiatric Association considers antisocial personality disorder to be a diagnosis for adults only. For patients who are younger than eighteen, the *DSM-5* directs clinicians to a separate category called "conduct disorder," a label that can confuse rather than clarify their understanding. This disorder is marked by persistent violations of social norms and the rights of others. Symptoms include destructiveness, lying, truancy, vandalism, stealing, the torturing and killing of animals, verbal and physical aggression, cruel and damaging behavior toward people, and the absence of guilt and remorse.

If you are the parent of a child who has been labeled with conduct disorder, in order to cope, you need to be aware of the complicated and somewhat baffling way this diagnosis is conceptualized by most mental health professionals. The *DSM* catalogs the following fifteen behaviors as its observable symptoms:

- Often bullies, threatens, or intimidates others
- Often initiates physical fights
- Has used a weapon that can cause serious physical harm to others (e.g., a bat, brick, broken bottle, knife, gun)
- Has been physically cruel to people
- Has been physically cruel to animals
- Has stolen while confronting a victim (e.g., mugging, purse snatching, extortion, armed robbery)

- Has forced someone into sexual activity
- Has deliberately engaged in fire-setting with the intention of causing serious damage
- Has deliberately destroyed others' property (other than by fire-setting)
- Has broken into someone else's house, building, or car
- Often lies to obtain goods or favors or to avoid obligations (i.e., "cons" others)
- Has stolen items of nontrivial value without confronting a victim (e.g., shoplifting, but without breaking and entering; forgery)
- Often stays out at night despite parental prohibitions, beginning before age 13 years
- Has run away from home overnight at least twice while living in parental or parental surrogate home (or once without returning for a lengthy period)
- Is often truant from school, beginning before age 13 years

Conduct disorder can be diagnosed in a child younger than ten ("childhood-onset type") if he or she demonstrates even one of these "major misbehaviors." Diagnosis after ten years of age ("adolescent-onset type") is considered if a child has exhibited three or more of these behaviors in the preceding twelve months, and at least one has been observed within the preceding six months. In other words, when diagnosing older children and adolescents, a clinician looks for a clear pattern of extreme misbehavior. A young child who pulls the dog's tail, or a teenager who tends to be late for curfew or who gets angry and sometimes talks back to his or her parents, is not showing a clear pattern of extreme misbehavior and does *not at all* belong in the extreme category of conduct disorder.

Viewing conduct disorder and sociopathy as two distinct disorders is not helpful for parents—or for clinicians, who definitely can attest that sociopathy does not spring forth new and full-fledged on an individual's eighteenth birthday. Unfortunately, well-meaning professionals do not wish to label any child with an especially ominous diagnosis that will certainly follow that child into the future, even if it is accurate. However, we can note that conduct disorder sounds very much like sociopathy, with the exception that some of the specified behaviors (in particular, those having to do with truancy and ignoring parental prohibitions) are more germane to children and adolescents than to adults. The central psychological feature of both sociopathy and conduct disorder is the absence of an age-appropriate sense of conscience, and both conditions are diagnosed by assessing the pathological behaviors enabled by this core deficiency.

Furthermore, longitudinal research indicates that at least 60 percent of individuals diagnosed with "adolescent-onset type" conduct disorder (diagnosed after the age of ten) will go on to manifest antisocial personality disorder as adults. Children who are diagnosed with conduct disorder before the age of ten are even more likely to become sociopathic adults. In fact, in order to make a formal diagnosis of antisocial personality disorder in an adult, there must be evidence of a previous conduct disorder, and this disorder must have begun before the person reached the age of fifteen. (In other words, something must have been amiss since childhood to qualify an adult for the antisocial personality disorder diagnosis.)

There is a subset of young people diagnosed with "adolescent-onset type" conduct disorder whose antisocial behaviors decrease substantially or even cease when adolescence is left behind, meaning that the individuals in this smaller group (about 40 percent of those first diagnosed in adolescence) are *not* diagnosed with antisocial personality disorder in adulthood. In the future, perhaps we will find that some of the adolescents we now diagnose with conduct disorder suffer from different problems altogether, problems that emanate from changeable environmental and developmental pressures during the difficult adolescent stage of life, rather than from a permanent core deficiency. When the diagnosis of conduct disorder is refined to exclude adolescents who are simply "acting out" in difficult circumstances or reacting to extreme pressures from gangs, drugs, poverty, and the violence around them, perhaps psychologists and psychiatrists will be able to remove the divide between sociopathy and "true" conduct disorder.

In the meantime, researchers have uncovered what may well be the deciding factor between a conduct disorder child who becomes an adult sociopath and one who ultimately does not. Unsurprisingly, this research leads once more to the inability to bond emotionally: we now have strong reason to believe that the presence of a *callous and unemotional interpersonal style* identifies a subgroup of antisocial and aggressive children within the more inclusive diagnosis of conduct disorder. In an extensive review of the research, psychologist Paul Frick of the University of New Orleans and neurologist Stuart White of the National Institute of Mental Health state that "callous-unemotional (CU) traits (e.g., lack of guilt, absence of empathy, callous use of others) seem to be relatively stable across childhood and adolescence and they designate a group of youth with a particularly severe, aggressive, and stable pattern of antisocial behavior. Further, antisocial youth with CU traits show a number of distinct emotional, cognitive, and personality characteristics compared with other antisocial youth." These characteristics include lower overall anxiety, abnormalities in responsiveness to punishment cues, and diminished responsiveness to distress cues in others.

While there is still more study to be done to refine our understanding of callous-unemotional individuals, Frick and other experts have maintained that the American Psychiatric Association should include the phrase "with significant callous-unemotional traits" as a "specifier" for a subcategory within the diagnosis of conduct disorder. The increasingly apparent need for such a specifier is underscored by the findings of a report published in 2012 in the United Kingdom, in the *Journal of the Royal Society of Medicine*, which concluded that the antisocial behavior of children with callous-unemotional traits may have a genetic link absent in conduct disorder children who do not show such traits. The genetics of this callous-unemotional condition are now thought to be associated with abnormal brain development.

Childhood conduct disorder is caused by an accumulation of factors that work together to engender pathological functioning. About 50 percent of the risk factors are neurological and genetic, and about 50 percent are environmental. These environmental influences include maternal malnutrition; early exposure to lead and other toxic substances; family involvement in antisocial behaviors; child abuse; and, most notably, a larger culture that models and rewards aggressive individualism, power over others, dog-eat-dog strategies, and "winning."

Child abuse has a deeply negative effect on virtually every aspect of a child's psyche and functioning. However, to say that child abuse is the *cause* of conduct disorder would be inaccurate; rather, abuse is one factor among many suspects. In 1994, a study was published in which abused and neglected children were matched with non-victimized children and followed into adulthood. In total, 694 people were assessed as adults, and the researchers found that significantly more of the subjects who had been abused and neglected in childhood met the study's criteria for sociopathy than did the non-abused subjects (13.5 percent versus 7.1 percent, respectively). But, looked at differently, these results mean that 86.5 percent of the abused children did not grow up to be sociopaths, and 7.1 percent of the comparison group of children did become sociopaths, despite not having been abused. In other words, *childhood abuse is neither a sufficient nor a necessary precursor of sociopathy.*

This is crucial information for the parents of conduct disorder children, who, in addition to the other torments they suffer, are often painted as child abusers. The notion that these parents are necessarily abusive is simply incorrect. And, as one mother wrote to me, "The parents are quite often blamed for creating the sociopath in the first place. Many of us (probably the majority) are just as victimized as the other people in their lives."

THE CALLOUS-UNEMOTIONAL BRAIN

Neurological factors have been more widely studied in adult sociopathy, where the research points to functional and even structural differences in the brain, particularly in the regions of the insula, the anterior and posterior cingulate cortex, the amygdala, the parahippocampal gyrus, and the anterior superior temporal gyrus (areas around the midline of the brain), and the orbito-frontal cortex (a region of the prefrontal cortex that is situated immediately behind and above the eyes). Collectively, these interconnecting limbic and paralimbic structures are referred to as the *paralimbic system*. The limbic system is involved with instinct and mood, controlling basic emotions and drives. The paralimbic system is involved in motivation, self-control, goal seeking, and the processing of one's own emotions and emotional input from the outside world.

Electrophysiological and brain imaging studies of emotional processing in sociopaths have led cognitive neuroscientists to conclude that *the neural circuitry involved in the paralimbic system of the brain is either completely dysfunctional or drastically under-functioning in sociopathy*. Why this problem in neural circuitry occurs is not yet known, but it is thought to be the result of a heritable neurodevelopmental difference that can be either slightly compensated for or made worse by child-rearing and/or cultural factors.

In 2010, researchers from the criminology, psychiatry, and psychology departments at the University of Pennsylvania sought to provide a formal test of the already widely accepted hypothesis that sociopathy has a neurodevelopmental basis. Using magnetic resonance imaging (MRI), they found that a well-known anatomical sign of faulty paralimbic development, called cavum septum pellucidum (CSP), is associated with sociopathy. The CSP is a slit-like, fluid-filled space of variable width located deep inside the brain, at the midline, between the two cerebral hemispheres. It is present in all human fetuses after about the twelfth week of gestation, but in 85 percent of fetuses it begins to close during approximately the twentieth week, and is completely fused by three to six months after the birth of the baby. This closure of the CSP is attributed to the normal, rapid development of the nerve fibers on the surface of the hippocampus, the amygdala, and other midline structures of the brain. Less robust development of these structures (in other words, faulty paralimbic development) interrupts the fusion process and results in the preservation of the CSP into adulthood. In this study, adult subjects with the CSP had significantly more sociopathic personality characteristics, and a history of significantly more sociopathic behaviors, than did adult non-CSP subjects, providing the first formal confirmation that early faulty development of the paralimbic system is associated with sociopathy.

As they began their human study, the University of Pennsylvania investigators were prompted by animal research to propose the cavum septum pellucidum as a "marker" for sociopathy. This much earlier research, involving rodents, rhesus monkeys, and various carnivores, had found that anomalies of the septum pellucidum were associated with increased aggression. (In light of what we now understand about the neurological aberration in sociopathy, these findings raise the broader question of whether nonhuman animals can be "sociopathic"—a question that has yet to be answered.)

The normal human brain applies special emphasis to emotional input from the outside world. Neuroscientists have found that the underdeveloped paralimbic system of the human sociopathic brain fails to support this activity. The normal brain pays speedier and stronger attention when confronted with emotional words (love, sadness, fear) or physically apparent emotion, which is a very adaptive reaction for our highly social and interdependent species. When sociopaths see or hear such words, or witness such reactions, their brains place no faster or greater emphasis on this emotional input than on neutral (non-emotional) words and events. When faced in the laboratory with tasks involving emotional language, adult sociopaths and adolescents with antisocial behavior problems are less facile at processing emotional words than are non-sociopathic adults and adolescents.

Sociopathic adults also do not show the same pattern of startle responses that normal adults quite reliably display while viewing evocative emotional pictures. Laboratory tests using simple tasks show that normal individuals are distracted by the presence of emotional pictures; not so for sociopaths, whose ability to attend to a neutral task is unaffected by emotional stimuli. And individuals prone to antisocial behavior show deficits in recognizing facial displays of emotion, especially expressions of fear. This shortfall in processing facial expressions reflects the fact that sociopaths suffer from a dysfunction in the amygdala, a part of the limbic system involved in many basic emotion-related functions, including the immediate identification of fear and other emotions.

Upon presenting subjects with tasks that require emotional processing, several functional imaging studies of sociopathic brains have noted *increased* activation in the dorsolateral region of the prefrontal cortex, an area involved in higher cognition. This observation suggests that sociopaths must calculate emotions such as love and caring—and even the anxiety and fear they love to cause—by using their intellect, much in the way the rest of us work out math problems. Together, these brain studies indicate that the recognition of any emotion is not instantaneous for sociopaths, as it is for non-sociopaths; instead, other people's emotional reactions, even the ones we would consider "obvious," must be worked out intellectually.

The neurodevelopmental defects in sociopathy have profound implications for the sociopath. Research indicates that the resulting overall *deficit in the preferential processing of emotion*—the metaphoric "hole in the brain" referred to in the previous chapter—accounts for the sociopath's inability to understand emotions automatically and failure to attach emotionally to other people. Since conscience is a response based in emotional connectedness to others, this inability to bond emotionally makes it impossible for the sociopath to feel conscience. In other words, the lack of a moral sense flags an even deeper and more tragic deficiency: the consciencelessness of the sociopath is rooted in neurological lovelessness.

Sadly, magnetic resonance imaging studies in the United States, England, and Germany indicate that many conduct disorder children and adolescents have brain abnormalities that substantially resemble the anomalies observed in adults with antisocial behavior, and exhibit the same blindness to distress-based social cues.

A 2008 German study, which looked at early-onset conduct disorder in boys, found *reduced gray matter volume* (by an average of 6 percent, compared with normal boys) in the left orbito-frontal region and in both temporal lobes, including the left side

of the amygdala and the hippocampus. In 2013, a British neuroimaging study of girls reported findings that were largely consistent with the data for the boys. This data indicates that—over
and beyond the functional differences—there may be actual
structural differences between the brains of callous-unemotional
children and those of normal children.

DIAGNOSING SILAS

Cold, calculating children certainly do not fulfill our conceptions of childhood innocence. Because this topic is such an emotional one, it is crucial for all of us, mental health experts
included, to hold clearly in our minds that conduct disorder
children who later "become" sociopaths are not filled with "evil"
or possessed. Rather, they suffer from a profound *deficit*: they are
neurologically unable to experience love and conscience. If we
can have the courage to view conscienceless children with un-
clouded eyes, we will be able to deal more effectively—and perhaps more compassionately—with them, and with the destructive
behaviors that arise from their condition.

Unfortunately, mental health professionals offer the parents
of these children only the euphemistic, misguided label of "conduct disorder." The parents are left quite alone in a frightening
situation with a makeshift and circular label accompanied by little explanation and even less constructive advice.

Imagine that Silas's heartbroken mother at last gathers the
courage to seek a psychiatric diagnosis for him after learning he had prowled their neighborhood after the death and

destruction of Superstorm Sandy. She is desperate to find something, anything—an explanation or perhaps just an unambiguous label—that might allow her to make sense of her child's strange and frightening behavior. She knows that something is dreadfully wrong with Silas, and she wants more than mere handholding from the expert she consults. What she wants is the truth.

After Silas is professionally evaluated, his mother will probably be told that he has a conduct disorder. The condition will be explained to her, and she will agree that Silas has many of the behavioral symptoms the doctor has listed. (She knows only too well that Silas manipulates and lies, is cruel to people and to animals, and never shows remorse.) But the mother will *not* be told that Silas may be a young sociopath; he cannot be given the adult diagnosis. Worse, a "callous-unemotional" distinction does not yet exist in the *DSM-5,* leaving this struggling mother without a true gauge for her son's emotional deficit.

If Silas's mother is ever told that he is sociopathic, this revelation will occur only when he is an adult, with a long path of destruction winding behind him. Many parents of children with conduct disorder, especially childhood-onset type, are left to feel that they are losing their minds. As young as two, a callous-unemotional child may begin to show temperament problems such as hyperactivity, impulsivity, irritability, and poor attachment. As these problems worsen, parents—even normal parents with the best of intentions—tend to get swept into an accelerating downward spiral. As the child grows increasingly noncompliant, the exhausted parents either give in to the child or intensify punishments. If they give in, the child's bad behavior is rewarded and strengthened. If they are physically punitive, the child gains role models for aggressive behaviors and soon begins his own campaign of aggressiveness, in time becoming much better at it than his parents ever could be. In this way, the parents of a conduct disorder child are damned if they do and damned if they don't, and often become anxious, ashamed, depressed, and despairing.

Fearing a public incident, the parents are reluctant to leave home, and gradually become cut off from the community. This isolation nearly always deepens their depression and sense of shame. And deterioration in the parents' functioning means that the other children in the family are seriously affected and may develop psychological problems of their own, no matter how many padlocks are placed on their doors to protect against physical violence.

Later in life, many remorseless children will learn how to isolate their victims socially and then convince them they are going crazy. Long before that time comes, we allow conduct disorder children to do the same to their families by our withholding important information. Emphasizing the truth to parents—that true conduct disorder is more than a disorder of conduct, but a disorder of *conscience*—causes pain at first, but in the end gives clarity and thus significant relief to caregivers at their wits' end.

It is my hope that reading the information provided here—difficult as it is for the heart to accept—will afford some insight and relief to parents who have been left alone with frantic questions concerning their children and growing doubts about their own sanity. Readying parents for the future is particularly important, because children who have no conscience do not stop being frightening and burdensome when they reach the age of eighteen. To the contrary, their actions only become more sophisticated and more disastrous for their families. Far into the adulthood of the sociopath, parents still nurture the hope that their child will "get better," and typically he or she repays them with an endless run of Kafkaesque episodes for which they feel somehow culpable. These waking nightmares tend to culminate in an incident, or a set of incidents, so disturbing that the parents realize they must either separate their lives from their adult child's or accept a continued lifetime of shocks and heartache. Unfortunately, they're also faced with the reality that separating completely from their own child, even a conscienceless one, also creates permanent heartache. This is an agonizing decision, one that no parent should have to make. And the overwhelming challenges do not end there; after the sociopath moves out (or is thrown out), the parents must somehow salvage the rest of their lives and continue to protect their other children.

Whenever I think about those other children—the sociopath's siblings, who are in danger throughout their lives—I tend to recall the following account. This story is not newsworthy. No one actually dies in it (yet). No one goes to prison. Some of the cruelties described may not even be illegal. Still, I find this story to be especially haunting:

> *My 21-year-old son Frank is blind, and I'm so proud of how he has coped with it. He makes his way through the house with ease, and can even play piano. But at this point, any praise or support from me or his father can't override his disdain for us. He has been turned against his own parents by his older sister, Gina. She has been very attentive to Frank in the past few years to win his favor. And she feeds him endless lies about his father*

and me. An outsider might see her as a good sister, but that's only because she turns on the politeness to fool them. They don't see her evil nature. No one would believe that she once locked the little boy who lived next door in the trunk of our car. She uses Frank's blindness to control and mock him. One day she dressed him in a white shirt that she had written obscenities on, then took him shopping. When a police officer approached Frank and questioned him, Gina feigned ignorance and somehow convinced him that we had written on the shirt. We watched in disgust as Gina flirted with the policeman, who clearly was skeptical of me when I said I didn't know anything about it. Once Gina took Frank into the city, saying they were going to a concert, then abandoned him at a train station. He has a cellphone and knows how to use it, but she made sure it was dead. He blamed us.

Manipulating Frank was full-time work for Gina. She never made any attempt to get a job, even though she did well in college and could certainly work. Instead, she tried to convince Frank to leave home and live with her in an apartment, using money she had made by selling the family silver on eBay. When we protested, she went to the police and accused us of physically abusing Frank. There were bruises on Frank's arms, and Gina told the police that my husband had caused them, and that he and I hit Frank all the time. But Gina's deviousness didn't work that time. Frank remembered that his father hadn't been home the day he was supposedly hit, and his father had called him that day. The long-distance call could be verified on his cellphone. Gina was finally caught, but still she kept trying to deny that she was the one who injured Frank. She finally left home at this point. Frank was traumatized. He had been conditioned to trust only his sister, and now he didn't know who to trust. He withdrew into himself and we haven't been able to bring him back to the wonderful boy we know he can be.

This story illustrates that sociopaths can spot the easy marks—the weak, the young, the poor, the physically and intellectually challenged. And, when one is seeking a victim for a cat-and-mouse game, who is more accessible than a member of one's own family? It also highlights that many sociopathic crimes cannot be prosecuted. It is not illegal to make one's brother unwittingly wear a shirt with curses on it. Frank's parents could not get so much as a restraining order from the court.

We know that Gina has no internal control system; her lack of conscience will allow her to do anything at all without experiencing even a glimmer of guilt or remorse. Putting all the pieces together, we (and her terrified mother) realize that she can, at any moment, do anything she wishes to her family, as long as she keeps her activities under the rather weak radar of the U.S. justice system.

TREATMENT: POSITIVE CONTINGENCY MANAGEMENT

"When you love someone who can't form an attachment, it just hurts so much," one reader wrote to me.

It is a sentiment I have heard more times than I can count. Parents are sorrowful and desperate to cure their conduct disorder children—to give them a normal, connected emotional life—and, even more painfully, are terrified when they ponder what the future may hold if their children do not change.

If you are the parent of a conduct disorder child, you may be aware of a number of treatments offered by residential schools, centers, and camps that claim they can "fix" him or her. Such programs subscribe to the idea that the behavior of conduct disorder children can be lastingly corrected through a long-enough stay (typically 90 to 120 days) in a setting of coercive behavioral regulation. Authority figures enforce rigid rules and schedules, and assign punishments for noncompliance. If you have tried one or more of these programs, you know they did not "fix" your child. After the child's homecoming, there may have been a few days, or even weeks, during which his or her behavior was better than before, but the improved behavior soon disintegrated, and the original antisocial behavior resumed. A swift relapse occurred because the core disorder, the absence of conscience, cannot be repaired by any known treatment, and it is this central deficit that allows the alarming behavior to occur. The harsh fact is that, at present, there is no cure for true conduct disorder, just as there is no cure for sociopathy. There is simply no known way to create a conscience in an individual who does not have one.

Individual and group psychodynamic therapy, psychiatric hospitalization, boot camps, and shock incarceration are all ineffective, at best, and can make matters worse. Research has shown that treatments carried out with groups of conduct disorder adolescents tend to increase antisocial behaviors, especially when group members are allowed to engage in discussions of defiant and illegal activities. Moreover, there are no medications for conduct disorder. Many conduct disorder children suffer from ADHD (attention deficit hyperactivity disorder) as well, and medicines intended to treat ADHD are used, with some success, to treat hyperactivity, inattention, and impulsivity in children who have this dual diagnosis. However, to date, no class of medication has been successful in treating conduct disorder itself.

Parents of preadolescent children may be heartened to learn of a system that can sometimes moderate the observable symptoms of conduct disorder—the "major misbehaviors" themselves—and so impart some measure of peace to an overwhelmed family. This approach is directed more toward the parents than the child, and involves multiple training sessions in the skill of *positive contingency management,* which is essentially a teaching technique. Unlike the popular "treatments" just described, positive contingency management is evidence-based, meaning that its effectiveness has been tested and refined through systematic research.

A *contingency* is simply an "if/then" pairing (if you do that, then this will happen). In instinctive child-rearing, most contingencies occur naturally and contain a social reward: *If* the child puts the bread back into the cabinet, *then* the parent smiles at him—where putting the bread back is the positive behavior, and the parent's smile is the reward. In contrast, when the parent has been trained and is deliberately managing contingencies, the links from specific behaviors to specific rewards are announced in advance and clearly defined on a "points chart." Each behavior (independently brushing teeth, using the toilet, and so forth) has a value on the points chart, and each reward is listed with its "price" in points. Though the points menu may list some material items (seven points for a superhero sticker, fourteen points for a specific small toy, etc.), social rewards also are used (an extra game of catch with Mom and Dad, having an extra book read at bedtime, etc.). In addition, success is accompanied by parental praise and perhaps a hug.

Conduct disorder children are far less motivated than other children by social rewards. On a points chart for such children, meaningful rewards will be more often material and conspicuously gratifying to the child (favorite meals, coveted electronics, computer time, new clothing). Also, many of the behaviors that earn points for a conduct disorder child will be geared toward very basic pro-social and nonviolent conduct, such as being good (i.e., not yelling or shoving) during an entire car ride, using only "good" language during dinner, or behaving carefully (not throwing anything) when the new baby is in the room.

Typically, parent training in contingency management (sometimes called "parent management training" or PMT) is provided by child behavior therapists. One prominent form of this approach is the Kazdin Method, named for its developer, behavioral psychologist Alan E. Kazdin, director of the Yale Parenting Center and Child Conduct Clinic. Kazdin makes it clear that contingency management treats the child's defiant behaviors directly, rather than treating the underlying cause, but he emphasizes that more pro-social behaviors, fewer negative interactions, and less chaos in the home are invaluable changes all by themselves (as beleaguered parents can attest). From the following illustration of a Kazdin-style approach, we can begin to appreciate the considerable value to parents of dealing directly with disruptive behaviors, even when the callous-unemotional disorder itself is not treated:

> Mr. and Mrs. Smith have two children, an eight-year-old conduct disorder son, William, and a five-year-old emotionally healthy daughter, Amy. After dinner every evening, as the family tries to watch something lighthearted on television, William kicks little Amy, hard, and laughs at her when she cries. Amy has bruises on her legs. Then, as Mrs. Smith is putting Amy to bed, William pushes into the room, describes a horrible imaginary monster (with remarkable creativity, a new one every night) and tells Amy that, when she falls asleep, the monster will enter her room magically, through her closet. Mrs. Smith pleads with William to leave the room, but to no avail. Amy is scared to death and, on many nights, ends up sleeping in her parents' bed with them.
>
> At the advice of William's pediatrician, Mr. and Mrs. Smith attend parent effectiveness training and learn how to set up a contingency management program designed to change some of William's behaviors. They affix a poster-size points chart to a kitchen wall and buy gold stars to represent William's points. Four stars on the chart entitle William to a candy bar after school (one day), and eight stars entitle him to an extra half hour of video game time (one day); or, if William wants to save up his points and manages to accumulate twenty stars, his parents will buy him a new action figure. The rewards and their respective "costs" are displayed prominently at the top of the chart. Stars are affixed to the chart

beside clear, specific accomplishments that are listed with their value in points. Most of the accomplishments involve self-restraint: "not swearing at Mom or Dad for one whole day," "not threatening to hit Mom when it's time to take medicine," "not saying or doing anything that causes a class-mate to become upset or cry," "not lying to the teacher," and several others. The school, which provides its own social skills and academic programs for troubled kids, will contact the home at least once each school day, with a report. The value of each accomplishment is one point per day, except for two items that are each worth two points per day. These two-point items are "not kicking Amy or hurting her in any other way" and "not talking to Amy about monsters or any other scary ideas."

William takes to this "game" quickly, since, in addition to getting prizes, he can "win" against his parents; in other words, he can "make" them give him things they normally would not. The system feels artificial to William's parents, and they are saddened to be reminded that their approval by itself does not motivate William. On the other hand, the system works! William's behavior improves, both at home and at school. Day-to-day life is a little easier. Bedtime is calmer. The parents worry that this "contingency management" approach is unfair to five-year-old Amy, since good behavior is natural to her, and she does not get material prizes for it. Exactly because she is *not* a conduct disorder child, she is deprived of the special treatment William now receives. They decide to give her a special prize sometimes, too, when she is especially cooperative with them or shares especially well with her playmates. But, really, the best parts of this new system for little Amy are that she does not get kicked by an eight-year-old every single day, and she does not have to hear about a terrible monster every night, just when it is time to close her eyes.

William has always seemed to enjoy wresting pained emotions out of his family members and watching their distress. (He is a young "emotion-eater.") They are understandably relieved that he now spends some of his time thinking about his "points game" instead.

Overall, the most effective therapeutic approach to conduct disorder is a treatment package, similar to the one for William, that includes parent training in contingency management, involvement of the child's school in the parents' efforts, medication for ADHD if that disorder is present, and academic support and social skills training for the child through the school. This approach does not provide a cure for the underlying problem in true conduct disorder. Rather, all elements of such a package are aimed at instituting and supporting *behavioral change* in these difficult children. For example, social skills training at school can succeed in teaching the young conduct disorder child to say *hello* and *please* and *thank you* to other children, and to get their attention in ways other than grabbing them and pushing them to the ground. But such training alters behavior only; it can never instill, as the child's reason to be better-mannered, a genuine desire to have friends. (We can note also that there is a certain uncomfortable irony in providing social skills training to a child who is likely to be a diagnosable sociopath.) However, for the parents and teachers of conduct disorder children, there are times when not having to see other children tormented or assaulted is a triumph all by itself.

Because of our society's rapid advancement in medical knowledge and technologies, the discovery of a biological cause for any disorder, such as paralimbic dysfunction in the callous-unemotional brain, tends to raise the question: Can we repair it? Given the extraordinary plasticity of forebrain neural circuits, as demonstrated by brains that recover various functions after an individual has suffered a stroke or a traumatic injury, might there be a way to override the neurological deficit in the callous-unemotional brain—a cure for the empty space where love and conscience normally reside?

There may be hope that, in the future, neurobiologists will develop chemical methods to augment the brain's natural plasticity, enhancing the tendency of brain circuitry to form and be molded by a person's repeated experiences. Regarding his treatment approach to conduct disorder, behaviorist Alan Kazdin has remarked that "repeated practice helps lock particular behaviors into your child's repertoire of behaviors, a process that involves changes in the brain. . . . Recent technological advances in the study of the chemistry and structure of the brain have given science the capacity to see how this process plays out on the molecular level, but that research is still in its early stages. For now, suffice it to say we know that repeated practice changes the brain, and we're still trying to figure out exactly what those changes look like."

With a chemical enhancement of the brain's inherent plasticity, used in tandem with behavioral training that repeatedly induces positive social interactions, perhaps we could repair the features of the brain that make interpersonal bonding possible. With a more normally functioning paralimbic system, the child would learn social skills at school because he actually wanted friends, and behave well at home because pleasing Mom and Dad felt important to him. Newly equipped with the ability to bond emotionally, he would have his own internal reason to behave well toward others. His conduct disorder would be vanquished, along with his possible fate as a lifelong sociopath.

Imagine a world in which people who would have been sociopaths—shameless Ponzi schemers, ruthless white-collar criminals, the cruelest of the schoolyard bullies, family tyrants, and cold-blooded political leaders—had instead been medically assisted to experience emotional bonding from the time they were babies. With funding and scientific interest, methods for permanently changing the brains of callous-unemotional children can and should be studied, and such studies may well prove to be world-altering. However, such a breathtaking victory—the ability to create a neurological milieu for love and conscience in a previously unaccommodating brain—lies far in the future.

PROTECTING YOUR OTHER CHILDREN—AND YOURSELVES

The parents of callous-unemotional children are not allowed the luxury of waiting for extensive scientific advances. They must cope right now with a disorder that currently has no cure. One especially anxiety-laden duty is to explain their conduct disorder child's disturbing behavior to the other children in the family. Very often, the already overstressed parents dread this looming conversation and are far from certain they can handle it well. But there is no perfect way to explain a sibling's lack of conscience, and any opening you give your non–conduct disorder children to talk about experiences that frighten and bewilder them will give them substantial relief. And there are some age-appropriate guidelines you can use in order to comfort your children and help them make sense of their conduct disorder brother or sister.

Mainly, the depth of the conversation should be governed by the child's own moral-developmental level. Under the age of about ten, most normal children view the difference between a wrong action and a right action as whether or not the behavior was punished by an authority figure. Because a normal child is emotionally bonded with his or her caregivers, receiving a punishment from Mom or Dad carries great weight and is often distressing—even if the punishment is a seemingly mild one, such as being told in an angry tone, "Stop that! That's bad!" Children in this young age group are very serious when they distinguish between wrong and right according to this punished/not punished criterion, and may react quite emotionally to a parent's anger and the associated pronouncements of "bad" and "wrong." (Many parents can recall a time when a young child, upon being chastised, simply curled up and cried.) And so, though adults may consider the young child's conception of right and wrong to be naive, parents must respect their child's way of thinking and feeling during any discussion, and most particularly during a discussion about a callous-unemotional sibling. When explaining conduct disorder to a normal child under the age of about ten, you will be more clearly understood if you speak in terms of punishment.

To illustrate, here is a bedtime conversation between a mother and her six-year-old daughter, Cara. Sitting on Cara's bed, they begin a discussion about Cara's ten-year-old conduct disorder sister, Nicole:

CARA: Remember yesterday? Nicole took the chains off the swing so I couldn't use it, and then she laughed at me, and you got mad and made her go in the house. You made her stay there, all the way to dinner.

MOM: Yes, I remember. You were very upset about the swing—and about being laughed at.

CARA: And you punished her.

MOM: Yes, I did. What Nicole did was wrong. She did it twice before, and I gave her two warnings. So, when she did it yesterday, I made her go back in the house.

They are silent for a moment, and then—

CARA: But . . . she did it again. She took the chains off again.

MOM: She did? When?

CARA: Today.

MOM: Oh, I'm so sorry, Cara. Tomorrow, I'll come outside with you while you're on the swing set. I'll be right there with you.

CARA: But I don't understand. Why did she do it again? You punished her for it.

There is another silence while Mom takes a deep breath. Then, finally—

MOM: When you get punished for something, you feel upset, right?

CARA: Yeah. I get really upset. It hurts me, I mean inside. It's . . . I don't know . . .

MOM: I know what you mean. When I was a kid, getting punished made me hurt inside, too. It feels bad for most people, I think. But Nicole is different in that way. Getting punished doesn't hurt her—at least, not the way it hurts you and me. That's why getting punished doesn't teach her anything. I mean, it doesn't make her not do it again.

CARA: All my friends get really upset when they get punished.

MOM: I know. But Nicole is different.

CARA: Well, when will she stop being different?

MOM: I think she may always be that way.

CARA: Can't we do something to make her not that way?

MOM: No, there's nothing we can do about how Nicole is. Nicole is Nicole, just like you are you, and I am me. The thing you always have to remember is . . . it's not your fault. Cara, can you promise me? Promise you'll always remember that it's not your fault?

CARA (looking at her mother curiously): Okay. I promise I'll remember that.

MOM: It's okay, sweetheart. I'll remind you sometimes. Will it be okay if I remind you?

CARA (tired of this subject for now): Can I go on the swing set
tomorrow?
MOM: Absolutely you can. I'll be right there with you.

One or two more conversations like this one—simply ac-
knowledging that her sister is different, and that anger and punishment do not hurt her feelings or make her stop doing
"wrong"—may substantially help Cara during a childhood full
of encounters with her sister. Now, from someone she trusts, she
has heard the straightforward message that Nicole is different
when it comes to matters of right and wrong, and that when
Nicole torments Cara, it is not Cara's fault. Mom's message will
help Cara feel less painfully confused when Nicole is cruel to her,
and inoculate her somewhat against Nicole's attempts to play
with her feelings.

Your discussions with an older child can be more nuanced.
Most normal children ten or older have matured past the point
of defining bad behavior as that which is punished, and have
developed a regard for societal and family rules ("Do not hurt
people"; "Do not steal"; "Lying is wrong"; etc.). For these children, the rules have become important in and of themselves, and
breaking the rules is the definition of bad behavior. At this stage,
the normal child will feel guilty when he or she is "bad" (has
broken a rule), whether or not the infraction is discovered and
punished. If your child has reached this level of development, he
or she will be able to participate in a discussion of *conscience*.

Let us imagine that Cara is twelve, rather than six, when her
mother first decides to discuss with her the callous-unemotional
nature of her older sister. Nicole, now sixteen, has just stolen

Cara's new shoes and hidden them—the extra-nice shoes that Cara saved up her allowance for a long time to buy. This strange act of Nicole's is only the most recent in a long line of incomprehensible and cruel acts intended to play havoc with Cara's emotions. A frantic search ensues, and when neither Cara nor her mother can find the shoes, Cara starts to sob. This situation is the last straw. During the past year or so, her mother has seen Cara become more and more depressed. She seems to lose a little more of her self-esteem with each passing day. Her mother was hoping that Cara's mood might be buoyed a little if she could save up her money and buy those shoes all by herself. And now Nicole has taken them. Mom feels like sobbing, too.

With more anger than either child has ever heard in her voice, she tells Nicole that, unless she produces the shoes immediately, she will be grounded for two weeks, though the mother is all too aware that grounding Nicole will result in an exhausting two-week battle.

To Mom and Cara's surprise, Nicole does not take this moment to proclaim that she is innocent. Instead, she looks calmly at Cara and says—

"Basement."

Cara races down the stairs to find her prized shoes.

Nicole calls down to her, "Behind the washing machine."

A few seconds pass, and then Cara cries out, "Oh no! Oh no! Why did she do this?"

Alarmed, Mom shouts down to her, "What's wrong, Cara?" But she feels that, somehow, she already knows.

"She broke the heels off! Why did she do this, Mom? She broke the heels off my shoes!"

Nicole is smiling broadly, as if she had just won a round of Texas Hold'em.

The mother wonders for the thousandth time how she and her husband could have raised gentle Cara and, in the very same home, this firstborn child who stole money and jewelry, viciously injured the family dog, attempted to set house fires, and lied constantly.

Mom vows to herself that this time she will have "the discussion" with Cara, and at bedtime that night she and her twelve-year-old daughter have a conversation that brings some relief to both of them. They talk about how awful their consciences would make them feel if they were to do some of the things Nicole has done.

"Cara, how would you feel if you intentionally destroyed something of Nicole's that she cared about a lot?"

"I'd feel incredibly guilty."

"Me, too."

Mom says she thinks of conscience as a voice inside her heart that will not stop making her feel guilty and unhappy if she hurts someone, even accidentally. Then, Mom explains to Cara that her sister does not have a conscience: Nicole does not have that voice inside her heart.

Cara thinks about this for a moment and then asks, "Does that mean Nicole never feels guilty about *anything*? That's too weird. I can't even imagine that."

"That's exactly right—she never feels guilty about anything," Mom says. "And I can't imagine it, either."

The day after this discussion, Cara comes to her mother and

discloses something she has not told her before because she thought feeling frightened about it meant she was being a baby: Nicole has been trying to convince Cara to try some of the cocaine Nicole keeps under the pajamas in the bottom drawer of her dresser.

"There's a whole bunch of it in there," Cara says, lowering her eyes guiltily.

Mom steadies herself and then tells Cara how glad she is that the two of them can talk together now, instead of Cara trying to deal with things like this all alone. She hugs her twelve-year-old for a very long moment and tells her how strong she is to resist so much pressure from her older sister.

Cara feels like something terrible has been lifted from her shoulders.

"Trying to get me to do that," she asks, "is that something Nicole does because she doesn't have a voice in her heart?"

"Yes, it is," Mom replies sadly, without trying to sugarcoat her answer.

There can be lasting repercussions from unexpected conversations like this. What recourse could Cara and Nicole's parents take? In this fictional scenario, they send Cara to her grandparents' house for safety, flush Nicole's cocaine down the toilet, and have a tearful, long-overdue discussion about getting Nicole out of the house when she is eighteen, as soon as she is legally an adult. In the past, she has run away from home on a number of occasions, often for days at a time, but they feel certain she will never move out permanently, not unless they make her leave. Living at home is just too easy.

Will they really have the emotional strength, less than two years from now, to force her out against her will? On the other hand, can they hold out that *long*? And more important, can Cara? Maybe they can still contact the therapist Nicole's doctor recommended years ago, when Nicole was first diagnosed with what he called conduct disorder.

In addition to needing a therapist, they may need a lawyer. The father feels sick to think they could require legal advice to deal with a sixteen-year-old. But what if Nicole is not just using drugs? What if she is selling them—from their house? They need to protect themselves. And even if the lawyer says they should, will he and his wife have the heart to turn their own child in to the police? What Nicole's father really believes is that after all the things Nicole has done to her family, they will do whatever the lawyer advises. He is correct about needing a lawyer, for even more reasons than he foresees. In many states, there are "lock-out laws" that penalize parents for locking out a child who is under the age of eighteen; when a child is involved in criminal behavior, the parents' legal situation is even more complicated. Evicting an adult child (eighteen and older) can be legally difficult as well. The laws vary by state and by country, and if you are considering closing your home to your child, a consultation with an attorney is wise. Just as important is contacting a therapist to help you deal with the emotional pain that parents in this situation often feel: loss, grief, a sense of failure, guilt over abandoning a child, a sense of relief, and guilt over the very fact that they feel relieved.

WHAT NOW? A GUIDE FOR PARENTS OF CONDUCT DISORDER CHILDREN

For the parents of conduct disorder children, I would like to emphasize a few pragmatic points from this chapter, along with some specific information to help you cope right now:

- Unless you are a child abuser, *your conscienceless child's condition is not your fault.* You have fallen into a desperately unfortunate circumstance, and you will need all of your strength to deal with it. Please do not spend your energy blaming yourself for a problem you did not cause and could not have predicted. If you are the parent of a callous-unemotional (conduct disorder) child, the following is the single most important point you can take from this book: *You did not do this to your child.*

- Individual and group psychodynamic therapy, psychiatric hospitalization, boot camps, and "shock incarceration" are all ineffective and may even worsen your callous-unemotional child's behavior. At present, the most effective therapeutic approach to conduct disorder in a younger child is a treatment package that includes contingency management (the Kazdin Method or a similar program), medication for attention deficit hyperactivity disorder (if your child suffers from ADHD in addition to conduct disorder), social skills training and academic support through the child's school, and involvement of the school to support the parents' efforts at home. I recommend that you seek out an experienced child psychologist to help coordinate this program. Your local school system may be able to help you find such a professional, who typically will specialize in behavioral psychology.

- Being the parent of a callous-unemotional child, adolescent, or adult is a psychologically overwhelming experience. I strongly recommend that you treat yourself with kindness and seek help for yourself. Allowing yourself to seek psychological help is just as important as setting up a program for your child, and perhaps more so. There are two online referral resources that I can recommend, through which you can search for therapists in your geographical area. One is a service of the American Psychological Association (www.apa.org): click on "Psychology Help Center" and then "Find a Psychologist." The other is the National Register of Health Service Psychologists (www.national register.org). When you get to "Find a Psychologist" on either site, you can filter by area of expertise. I recommend Post-Traumatic Stress Disorder or Acute Trauma Reaction.

- The presence of a callous-unemotional child creates pressures and anguish for the entire family. Though this is disturbing to contemplate, your other children may be affected by your callous-unemotional child for the rest of their lives. I recommend an open and ongoing discussion of these problems even with younger children, and more specific information (possibly using this book and other literature) for older children, certainly by their teen years. You will do your other children no favors by trying to "shelter" them from information about their experiences; failure to discuss their sibling's condition will only leave them to figure it out alone and to feel that perhaps they are crazy, just as you did. The most loving choice is an open discussion with them, in the age-appropriate ways illustrated in this chapter.

- At present, there is no cure. In many cases, a permanent separation between a family and a teen or young adult with conduct disorder is unavoidable. Again, please seek professional help for yourself in order to address the emotional pain and guilt that are very often a part of this situation.

HUMAN EVIL AT WORK

Sociopathic Coworkers, Bosses, and Professionals

"Are you suggesting that this is a knife I hold in my hand?"

—*Gaslight* (1944)

Angela was bored this morning, even more so than usual. To make matters worse, in a few minutes she had to meet with a new member of her staff, Kyle, to discuss his three-month review. She pulled up a review form on her computer and thought for a moment. She should have completed the form and written a paragraph or two about Kyle before now, but it was all so stupidly tedious. He seemed good at his job, and so far he had not given her any trouble. In fact, as she reflected on it now, he had not paid much attention to her at all. *Well,* she thought, *I bet I can change that.* This thought made her smile. She clicked boxes on the form, giving Kyle "Good" and "Excellent" marks all the way down the page, until she came to "Interacts well with staff";

on that item, she gave him an "Average" so that her answers would not be too uniformly good for her own boss to perceive them as thoughtful and honest. Then she hit PRINT.

She knew this very positive review would make Kyle happy. He would probably go straight home after work and tell the wife about it. Angela had heard he was a real family man. She smiled again.

When Kyle walked into her office, Angela took a good look at him. He was skinny but with nice broad shoulders, and she decided he was reasonably attractive. He was definitely nervous. She gave him a big smile, and he smiled back shyly.

"Come in, Kyle!" she said, and when he started toward the chair by her desk, she motioned for him to sit on the sofa instead.

"I think you'll find this is going to be a very friendly chat."

"That would be really nice, Ms. Woodson."

"Oh, Kyle, please. Call me Angela."

He smiled shyly again and sat down on the sofa, which was uncomfortably soft and low for him. He tried unsuccessfully to find a decent position for his legs. She walked across the room, making sure he got an eyeful of her swaying hips, and hooked the latch on the door, a simple but useful device she had installed herself on her first day in the office. Fastening it always made people feel a bit trapped, even though it was just a little clasp. She liked the effect. And, of course, no one ever got up enough nerve to ask her why she was locking the door.

She showed off her fine body again as she walked back to her desk, picked up the review she had just printed, and sat down beside Kyle, making sure to be just an inch or two within his personal space. Really, she was so good at these tactics that she felt like crowing. But that would have to wait. There was work to be done if she was going to win this first round with Kyle.

She handed him the form. "Here, Kyle. You can read this. I think you'll like what you see."

While he looked through the items on the form, she slipped off her heels and folded her legs up under herself. Now she was facing sideways, toward him, and somewhat closer than before.

"Wow," he said. "This is a wonderful review. Thank you so much. I really, really like this job, and I've been trying really hard."

"Well, it shows, Kyle. Your work is fantastic. I'm sure we can have a positive relationship here at Eastern. I hope you agree."

"I'd really like that, Ms. Woodson."

She placed her hand on his leg, just above the knee, and crooned, "Kyle, call me Angela." Then she moved over so their shoulders were slightly touching. He glanced at her sideways, bewildered.

Casting her eyes at the review he was gripping, she said, "I'm especially pleased with item four. See there—your attention to office policies. It's excellent." She leaned in still more, as if trying to read the form, and now more than her shoulder was pressing against him. *Dear God,* he thought, and turned bright red in the face.

At that moment, the buzzer sounded on Angela's desk. She said, "Damn," then got up and walked across the room in her stocking feet. Kyle stared incredulously at the abandoned high heels by the sofa.

"What is it?" she snapped at her assistant, followed by "Oh. Put him through." Then she said to Kyle, "You can go now."

Kyle's face was still red. As Angela's boss began to speak to her on the phone, she watched in amusement as he fairly sprinted to the door. He was so shaken that he fumbled for one very long moment with the simple little hook-and-eye latch before getting it loose and darting out of the office. *And so the game begins, Kyle,* she thought. *What fun.*

The boss wanted to talk about his pet project, an overly cautious new marketing scheme he had described a million times before that was completely uninteresting to Angela. However, chatting about the project did provide an opportunity to slather flattery on the boss, which she took advantage of, outrageously, for a full fifteen minutes. "Fantastic," "groundbreaking," *yada yada yada*. The boss loved it, and she knew he was beginning to think that maybe he loved Angela as well.

Now she was on a roll. When the conversation with her boss was done, she decided to go have a talk with Grace, an underling who was always especially fun to play with. Grace was excellent at her job, and she had what people sometimes referred to as a "good heart." Angela knew that Grace's coworkers were very fond of her and would like to come to her defense, but their concerns about losing their jobs made them afraid to speak up. Angela thought it was funny how the downturn in the economy had so effectively assisted her game.

She opened a desk drawer and took out an orange rubber wristband that had come with a donation request from a domestic violence agency. The band bore the exhortation TAKE A STAND. She had thrown away the plea for money but had kept the orange wristband, thinking she might find a use for it. Now she stowed it in her jacket pocket, put her shoes back on, and went out to the main office, where her twelve staff members sat at their desks, keyboards clicking. Grace's desk faced away, and Angela walked up behind her unnoticed.

"Grace!" she said in a loud, severe voice.

Grace jumped and swiveled around in fright. "Ms. Woodson! Do you need me?"

"It's almost lunchtime, isn't it, Grace?"

"Well . . . yes, I guess it is."

"Half the day is gone. What did you get done this morning?"

"What did I . . . Well, I finished answering those emails you told me to take care of."

"What emails? I never asked you to take care of any emails."

"Yes, remember? I was leaving yesterday, and you said that in the morning, I should—"

"No, I don't remember, Grace. Why do you make these things up when you know I'm going to call you on them? Or maybe you're confused because you don't know how to listen. Maybe you need to learn how to listen better. Do you think that could be it?"

"But I know you said—"

"And I said I didn't. Here, I'm going to help you remember about the listening."

Angela took the wristband out of her pocket and held it out to Grace, who looked at it with uncomprehending eyes.

"Whenever you see the bright orange band, I want you to remember to listen. Take it. Put it on."

Grace took the thing from Angela's hand and said, "But I don't really want to wear this."

"You see? You're not listening again. I didn't ask if you wanted to. Now put it on."

Grace was terribly angry, but fearing for her job—and fearing Angela—she squeezed her right hand through the rubber bracelet and stared down at her wrist. To her humiliation, she realized that she was about to cry again in front of her coworkers.

When Angela saw the first tear, she knew her mission had been accomplished. Satisfied for now, she looked around the room at all the defeated faces pretending not to see. She felt deliciously powerful.

THE NATURAL HISTORY OF HELPING

I imagine that, by now, you can readily assess Angela as a sociopath. And you can probably cite the symptoms that cause you to think so: her constant deceitfulness; her tendency to be bored; her desire to "play" with people and to make them jump; her irresponsibility, manipulativeness, and "charming" use of flattery; her use of sexuality as a means to an end; and her preoccupation with power, not to mention her general cold-bloodedness and calculating nature. In the workplace, where people are expected to help and cooperate with each other toward common goals, Angela shows zero interest in helping or cooperating, or in serving the group in any other way. Her only goals are her own selfish and strangely predatory ones.

Over eons, nature has hardwired the brains of mammals (definitely including us) with an adaptive predisposition to cooperate with others, and we can see just how profoundly pathological and odd Angela's sociopathic goals are by recounting the helping behaviors of some purportedly "subhuman" animals. I begin with the story of a young chimpanzee named Mike.

In the Kédougou region of the Republic of Senegal, in 2009, a group of poachers located a nine-month-old chimpanzee and abducted her. During the assault on her community, the mother of the infant was seriously injured by the poachers' dogs. The cruel abduction of a young animal is not an uncommon occurrence in Africa, but this instance was unusual in that a group of scientists was able to confiscate this chimp from her abductors, and successfully return her to her mother five days later.

The incensed anthropologists from Iowa State University, who were in Senegal to observe savanna-woodland chimpanzees in their natural habitat, named the baby Aimee and searched for her injured mother in the wild. They found her in a feeding tree with nine other chimpanzees and named her Tia. The researchers placed Aimee on the ground about fifty feet from the tree and retreated. As soon as the humans were a safe distance away, an adolescent male, Mike, whom the researchers knew to be about ten years old and unrelated to Tia, climbed down, retrieved little Aimee, and carried her closer to the base of the tree. Despite her injury, mother Tia quickly descended the tree, and Mike gave the baby to her. All of the other chimpanzees clambered down and gathered around Tia and Aimee, pant-grunting their greetings.

Holding Aimee close to her body, Tia rested for several hours along with the others. The researchers stayed on and watched from a distance. In the late afternoon, it was time for the chimpanzee group to move on. Because of the injury inflicted on her by the poachers' dogs, Tia was limping and could not keep up.

As she tried, her wound began to bleed, and she stopped frequently to examine it and wave away flies. Each time she rested, she placed Aimee on the ground close by her side and then picked her up again as she continued in her attempt to follow the group. About five minutes into the journey, noticing this, Mike returned to Tia, scooped up baby Aimee, and carried her during the rest of the trip. When the group reached its nest site, Tia took her baby back.

There are countless other accounts of animals helping each other (and us)—captive chimpanzees clenching their toes into fists and preparing to protect human caregivers from perceived threats, elephants being watchful nannies for the calves of other elephants, warthogs adopting the orphaned offspring of other warthogs, wild chimpanzees placing consoling arms around upset group members, rooks in the laboratory partnering to operate a feeding mechanism devised for two, wild ravens snatching prey from larger and fiercer animals by tag-teaming them, "go-between" macaques breaking up intragroup conflicts and keeping the peace, and on and on. Commenting on the weight of the evidence, primatologist Frans de Waal states unequivocally, "All species that rely on cooperation—from elephants to wolves and people—show group loyalty and helping tendencies." Ethologist Marc Bekoff and bioethicist Jessica Pierce write in *Wild Justice*, "The recent deluge of essays and research papers on cooperation shows that the more we look for cooperation in animals the more we discover its presence. And indeed, if you watch animals for any length of time, it's easy to see a good deal of cooperating and plain old getting along."

Because survival in the wild and ever-threatening world of our primeval ancestors was made much more likely by living in co-operative groups—and less likely by being completely apart from the help and protection of others—many evolutionists propose that natural selection favored individuals who exhibited non-zero-sum (win-win) behaviors such as friend-seeking, coopera-tion, and the avoidance of conflict within the group. The rudimentary limbic systems that began to evolve in the brains of our mammalian predecessors were extraordinarily adaptive. At-tachment, loyalty, and a tendency to cooperate kept our earliest forebears alive and reproducing.

I speak of nonhuman animals to emphasize a point about the human ones: when we as human beings help each other out and work together to get things done, we are only doing what comes naturally. Loyalty and helping tendencies are inscribed indelibly into our makeup. We are predisposed to cooperate with those who are close to us in our homes and workplaces, and to give assistance and support to them when they are in need. We have their backs, and they have ours. Sometimes we do these things gladly and sometimes grudgingly, but we almost always do them. Laziness and disloyalty to one's friends are seen as extraordinarily undesirable behaviors. Our distant ancestors knew this, and whisper it to us from deep inside the most primal parts of our brains. Normal social animals simply are not saboteurs.

The biologically prepared inclination to work together is the special magic and the possible salvation of social creatures—from tiny, vulnerable prehistoric rodents, to chimpanzees in their dwindling habitats, to us. By working together, human beings built the Twin Towers of the World Trade Center, and when evil—the empty hole of lovelessness—demolished them, people worked together again to plan and construct a meaningful memorial. Persisting in groups, people built the Golden Gate Bridge, the Hoover Dam, the Panama Canal. We cure lethal diseases collaboratively. We perform breathtaking symphonies, build great libraries of knowledge and imagination, and develop an endless array of brilliant technological advances by working in teams, by combining our forces. And if we could cooperate rationally and well enough, we might conceivably preserve our green planet and feed every woman, man, and child who lives on it.

We have not yet worked together rationally and well enough for several reasons, the most conspicuous being political and ethnic vendettas, warring religions, and greed. And another reason: not all human beings are inclined by their nature to cooperate. A loveless few see other people merely as living toys to be played with, schemed against, and dominated.

Findings about the social animals on our planet—and we are perhaps the most social of all—underscore how profound the sociopath's deficit is. To have no social sense, no emotional attachment to one's fellows, no inclination to help out—instead to be willing and able to plot sabotage and slash figuratively or literally at a group member, or at the group as a whole, often just for the fun of it—is to be psychologically distorted by an emotional hole unfathomable to the rest of us. When it passes near us, the shadow of human evil breathes an unforgettable chill wind. For us humans, discovering cold-bloodedness in a helper or a colleague or a "friend" can be a primally frightening experience. When we are victimized by conscienceless group members, coworkers, friends, or neighbors, an ineffable anxiety can freeze us in place, so strong is our own species-sense that some primordial code has been violated.

Despite our penchant for giving evil a name and a face, it is neither an entity outside of us nor a part of our normal human makeup. In the very large majority of circumstances, social creatures—the humans and the apes, the warthogs rooting in the savannas, the wolves howling in the forests—do not harbor a potential to commit evil against the group. Unless driven by a scarcity of survival resources, which is an overwhelmingly powerful motivator for all living things, they will almost never maim or destroy their own. To the contrary, they will help out, they will nurture, and they will cooperate with and protect their companions. That is the good news. The bad news is that, as we've discussed, some human brains contain a strange and profound deficit that allows the bearers of such brains to perform evil acts without guilt—sometimes with glee, in fact—and that the people who possess this alien gray matter live among us; look just like us; cause us worlds of trouble, pain, and loss; and will never change or stop by themselves. So, let us consider what *we* can do to stop them, in the place where most adults spend most of their waking time and where cooperation is imperative: at work.

COMPETITIVE BEHAVIOR IN SOCIOPATHY

After the publication of *The Sociopath Next Door,* I received a torrent of letters similar to the following one, concerning remorseless people in the workplace. Each and every one describes a situation in which a single individual has harmed the lives of at least one and often many kind, generous, caring, and loving people. The majority of these letters mention a sense of responsibility toward potential future victims, and also the fact that the passage of time alone has not completely healed the damage, though the victimization may have been brought to an end:

> *A ghost has haunted my marriage to Steven, since day one. I met him at an ad agency, where we were both account executives. After we had been going out a few weeks, he told me that he had been married to Paula, the chair of the department. The marriage had been pure hell for him. She did everything she could to isolate him. She would take his cellphone and delete messages from his friends, then text nasty messages to them as if from him. She made long scratches down the side of his car, then denied any knowledge of it. He was baffled why she even wanted to be with him. Despite his misery, Steven stuck it out for five years. Paula had some mysterious power over him. Although he tried to leave her many times, she reeled him back in. She went from apologizing profusely to threatening suicide. She blackmailed him by claiming she would post videos she had secretly taken of them having sex on the Internet if he dared to leave her. Finally, he got a divorce, three years ago.*
>
> *Paula's relationship to Steven was only the tip of the iceberg. She had apparently demeaned many other people at the agency. Still, she was promoted to Account Director, because she was good with clients and managed to hide her evil ways from the higher-ups. Meanwhile, she kept digging her claws into Steven*

and me while we were both looking for a new job. A few interviews he had scheduled were canceled abruptly. He later found out that she had called Human Resources and bad-mouthed him. She'd often make him work on accounts that required him to stay late, with her. It was then that she would tell him that I was two-timing him at every opportunity. Steven never believed her, thank God, but it stung.

It wouldn't stop even after our marriage, when we no longer worked at the agency. Steven couldn't seem to untangle himself from her web. He had to change his phone number because she called or texted him relentlessly. Then she somehow managed to get his new number and start all over again. The combination of evil and cunning was devastating us without letup. I'll never understand how such a person could maintain a successful career. It's as if she turned a switch on when she wanted to torment Steven, then off again when she had to resume a professional appearance. The "why?" of it was most puzzling of all.

Was Steven an easy mark for her? I sometimes wonder. With all her lies, she still could push his buttons. She got him to give her money after telling him she had totaled her car and had no collision insurance, an obvious lie. Then we found out that she had sold her car and bought a new one. He also found out that she had had affairs with a number of men at the agency, while she and Steven were still married.

I'm happy to report that Steven and I have found a great counselor who has helped us come to grips with the situation. We also now get together with people from the old agency who also were victimized by Paula to share horror stories and provide support. Somehow Paula found out about our counselor. She called her and trashed us, saying that we had emotionally abused her and driven her to consider suicide. We later found out that she had become totally alienated from her family. She had stolen from them, spread mean, false rumors about her married sisters having affairs. The worst thing of all was when she called the police (anonymously, but we know it was her) and claimed that Steven was the driver in a local hit-and-run case where a boy had been killed. It was a warm day and all the neighbors were outside as two policemen arrived at our house and questioned him, asking him to provide proof of his whereabouts that day.

We finally got a restraining order against Paula, and she has relented somewhat in her attempts to wreck our lives. But I fear this won't be the end of it. By now she is probably on another mission of destruction with some man she has managed to seduce. Being able to commiserate with others who have suffered her torment has helped. But I wonder what can be done to stop her.

Here, it is important to convey more about what truly socio-pathic victimization is like—and what it is *not* like. As we can begin to see from the story of Paula, ruthless individuals in the workplace do not tend to engage in ordinary competitive activi-ties. To the contrary, their behavior and the motivation for it are usually quite different from the motivations and competitive be-haviors that psychologically sound people exhibit from time to time.

Like cooperation and helping, competition is age-old, and in normal animals, just as in normal human beings, competitive (or *agonistic*) behaviors can be brutal when the motivation is survival-related. Crowded animals and animals in stressed habitats will fight one another for resources, sometimes forcing the actual exile of other group members. For example, researchers studying mongoose groups in Uganda have found that dominant female banded mongooses will chase, scratch, bite, and generally plague their younger pregnant relatives until the subordinate females are forced to depart from the group, leaving more resources for the pups of the dominant mothers. And, of course, even in non-stressed circumstances, animals and humans alike may battle, in one fashion or another, for dominance and desirable sexual partners. In humans, competition is sometimes physical but is more often—especially in the workplace—verbal or even just quietly mental.

All such fighting involves *goal-directed aggression*. In other words, normal competition has a comprehensible objective and is intended to enhance the aggressor's survival or well-being. One of the surprising giveaways of sociopathic behavior is that often it is not self-promoting in the usual sense. Typically, the socio-path "competes"—violently, verbally, sexually, or in some other way—for the exclusive purposes of diminishing and controlling others, such that sociopathic competition looks less like vying with another person for resources and advancement (normal be-havior in many work settings) and more like tormenting and attempting to damage another person just for fun (distinctly ab-normal and disruptive behavior in any work setting). Still more surprising is the fact that the sociopath's need to diminish and control, far from helping her out in the workplace, will often drive her to place her own survival or well-being in that setting at substantial risk. The startling truth is that, even if we wanted to do so, very few of us would enact such schemes because we know such actions might amount to social, professional, or financial suicide in the long run.

The unmoderated desire to make people jump is seldom productive, even for the person who holds the strings. For example, sending thousands of abusive texts and, as a department head, sleeping with various departmental underlings—these are far from self-promoting schemes. Rather, they are belittling, controlling, and essentially irrational things to do.

As perhaps the best illustration of a heartless tactic that has no self-promoting value, many of the letters I receive describe a situation in which someone has apparently decided to control another person by gaslighting her—in other words, by making the victim feel she is losing her mind. The expression is taken from the play *Gaslight,* popularized by the 1944 film in which a villain played by Charles Boyer attempts to guard the secret of his murderous past by playing sinister tricks on his new wife, Ingrid Bergman, encouraging her to believe that she is going mad. One of the tricks is to raise and lower the brightness of the gaslights in the house and make her believe she is imagining it. One of the most painful aspects of being gaslighted is that, from the perspective of other people, the tactic is so seemingly pointless and the victim's complaints so odd and paranoid sounding that the victim's frightening predicament is all but impossible to believe. Gaslighting is especially prominent in workplace situations. Of all the ways to diminish and control another person, causing that person to doubt her own perceptions and thoughts is among the most callous—and effective.

SOCIOPATHY IN A "CLOSED SYSTEM"

Many of the communications I receive illustrate the fact that, very often, the ruthless will choose the easy marks at work, the most vulnerable—those who already doubt themselves:

> *My problems started a few years ago, when I was separated from my husband and contemplating divorce. To help make ends meet, I got a job as a bar manager and part-time bookkeeper for a new pub that was opened by an acquaintance. I was befriended by one of the bartenders there, an attractive guy who was sympathetic to all the problems I was going through—my difficulties with my husband, my fears about the impact of a divorce on our two young daughters. Ryan opened up to me about his own difficult divorce, and I was impressed by what a great father he was to his three kids. He said he spent a lot of his free time with them. Also at the gym—he kept himself in great shape. We began hanging out together after work, talking, laughing, and drinking—he was such a good listener. Sometimes he would tell me how tense I was, and offer shoulder and neck massages. He said he was "wildly attracted" to me, but that he did not want to begin an affair unless I was officially divorced. I thought this was admirable. But sometimes after we'd been drinking he'd kiss me passionately, then push me*

*away, which drove me crazy. I began fantasizing about starting
a new life with him. He soon started telling me about his own
financial burdens—the struggle of paying child support. I grew
uncomfortable when he began asking me questions about how
much other people at the pub made, including our boss. When I
told him that I couldn't reveal any financial information, he
would grow cold toward me and pull away for a time before
warming up again. I felt increasingly pressured by him to reveal
private information. As time went on, he complained more
about the boss—the number of hours he was forced to work, for
too little money. He said our boss was taking advantage of me as
well. I knew his pay was fair, but I did speak to the boss about
giving him more time off. I did not want to lose Ryan's
friendship. I felt conflicted and confused, and began drinking
too much. Any time I asked him how he felt about me, he said
he still wanted me. He began asking me for "cash advances,"
which he said he would pay back soon. I never did this,
although I thought about it. I can't believe now how I fell for his
charms.*

*Ultimately, Ryan lost his job. I felt terrible, until he called
me up and blamed me! He was vicious, like an entirely different
person. He said he was going to report that I had sexually
harassed him. I was worried about being taken to court, and
didn't know what to do. I told my boss and some other workers
the truth about our relationship, which Ryan said was all in my
imagination. And he lied that I constantly trashed the boss and
coworkers, when in reality I always defended them against any
attacks. I left the job, mortified, and went back to my husband,
and am desperately trying to work things out. My husband and*

I are in couples counseling and I am also in therapy alone, trying to make sense of the person I had become. I can't believe how susceptible I was. I'm so ashamed, I want to move far away from this city. I feel that I was taken advantage of during an extremely vulnerable time in my life, and I wonder how I can ever trust anyone again. Including myself.

This story about a bartender and a bookkeeper illustrates many likely features of sociopathic behavior in a work setting:

- Flattering the victim
- Self-aggrandizement
- Attempts to appear kind and helpful
- Seductiveness
- Lying
- Inducing another person to take out-of-character risks
- The "pity play"
- Blaming
- Intimidation
- Cold-blooded betrayal

Further, the account demonstrates the victim's sense of failure and the debilitating loss of her self-esteem and much of her ability to trust anyone, including herself.

The relationship between the bookkeeper and the bartender occurred inside what I refer to as a "closed system": an isolated liaison known only to the two of them. Because she was increasingly insecure about and embarrassed by her own behavior, the bookkeeper did not discuss her situation with anyone. In fact, she participated in keeping the relationship a secret. Because abuse flourishes in secrecy and isolation, remaining in such a closed system in any area of your life will make you dangerously vulnerable to sociopathic exploitation. If you find yourself in a stressful and precarious closed system at work, I strongly recommend that you let in some oxygen by discussing this relationship with at least one person *in the outside world*. This person can be a close non-work friend, a family member, or a therapist. In your conversations, there is no need at all to use the term *sociopath* or any other formal language; simply describe what is going on at work. Also, do not expect your confidant to provide an immediate solution to your dilemma or even to form the same opinion as yours. Your goals are (1) to prevent an anxiety-inducing person from isolating you completely, and (2) to hear a caring voice, one that comes from outside of your own mind.

Opening the closed system to outside input is of crucial importance. Talking and being listened to will reduce your sense of panic, encourage you to think more objectively about what is happening, and provide you with the mental space to consider what you know about the sociopathic pattern, in case the other person in the formerly closed system does turn out to be a sociopath. And if the person under discussion wishes to keep you isolated and strongly objects to your conversations with anyone else, consider that a large red flag. The bookkeeper would have benefited greatly from cracking open the closed system she was in. And should Kyle and Grace, from the example at the start of this chapter, get together and compare notes about the seductive and frightening behaviors of their boss, Angela, they will feel less isolated and "crazy." Together, they might be emboldened to speak with other coworkers as well, about what is quite possibly a mutual problem. (Recall that the abusive Angela was very much aware that financial fears had isolated Grace from her coworkers, and that Grace's solitariness worked very much to Angela's advantage when tormenting her.)

To initiate a sociopathic pattern, the ruthless may pick the especially vulnerable, because, as we have just seen, this is horrifyingly easy. Sociopaths who have more power and resources themselves often will take aim at more challenging targets—individuals who are extremely accomplished in their careers—apparently because such people inspire envy and also because they supply greater sport. Such is the case in the following account:

> *Two years ago my life was ripped apart because of my boss, who convinced me with his charm and extravagant promises that he knew how to parlay my professional connections into grand success. I'm ashamed to say I was swayed by his passionate talk about how great and rich I could be. It all sounded so rational and foolproof. He used deception and lies to gain my trust and my money, then he crushed me with accusations of dishonesty when I began to see through him. It was no use trying to talk to him or get him to fix the damage he'd caused. In the end he tossed me aside like a piece of trash. It took a lot of courage for me to take him to court, and of course I wound up settling and not recouping a lot of the money I'd lost. How could I have been so gullible?*
>
> *We work in the same industry, so I have to see him at events and conferences. Once he glared at me from the audience while I was addressing a group. He is still bound up with my*

*professional life, and that unchangeable fact seems to keep me
from being able to move on. I feel powerless and ashamed, and
I'm reminded of that every day.*

How is it that sociopaths are so good at involving both vulnerable people and relatively powerful people in workplace and
professional tragedies? And why do emotionally normal employers hire them in the first place, and then keep them on, despite
the chaotic problems, extreme disadvantages to business, and
costly interpersonal pain they delight in fomenting? The answers
to these questions have to do with the fundamental nature of
sociopathy. Sociopaths do not view other people in the natural
way the rest of us do—as warm beings toward whom we spontaneously and inevitably have real emotional reactions, both negative and positive. Instead, the ruthless view others as game pieces,
pawns, or puppets who are there to be controlled. This odd, indeed nearly incomprehensible perspective on other human beings, along with an inability to experience guilt or shame, directs
the sociopath into certain power-thirsty strategies and predictable patterns in the workplace:

1. *Counterfeiting kindness and generosity.* As an initial power
   strategy at work, the sociopath will nearly always present
   him- or herself as kind and especially generous, just as the
   bartender presented himself to the bookkeeper, and just as
   Angela did to Kyle. Often, this sets the stage for the victim
   to be gaslighted into doubting his or her truer perceptions.

2. *Using the pity play.* After this charitable persona has been projected, often a ruthless person will attempt a manipulative "pity play" involving one or more claims that he himself is being victimized by someone else, just as the bartender claimed he was overworked and underpaid by his boss, and just as the woman at the ad agency, Paula, pointed her finger back at her ex-husband, Steve, even as she continued to abuse him.

3. *Calculating emotional soft spots.* Usually, sociopaths are invisible to us, because they look like us and are careful to behave as we do; but normal people are not at all invisible to sociopaths. To the contrary, sociopaths typically make a lifetime career out of reading other people, sizing us up emotionally and character-wise. In a work situation, a sociopath will calculate which individuals are most responsive to pity plays, and also where the interpersonal vulnerabilities are located—in other words, the emotional soft spots in his coworkers and superiors that he can push, causing people in the workplace to believe that they need him, sometimes desperately. The bookkeeper quickly came to feel that she needed the bartender, and only the bartender, for both love and self-validation, and indeed, a *yearning for self-validation* is one of the sociopath's preferred soft spots; it allows him or her to come to the "rescue" with false comfort and extreme flattery. The tactic of using emotional soft spots is commonly played out sexually—sleeping with someone higher on the organizational ladder being the most famous example—especially

if this will place a supervisor, boss, or colleague in a compromising position. All too frequently, sociopaths seem to hold mortgages on other people's lives.

4. *Cultivating a sense of indebtedness.* Through posing as a kind and generous person, and by sliding into an emotional vacuum and pretending to fill it, the sociopath creates a sense of indebtedness in a coworker or an employer. Sometimes a sociopath will actually generate a problem and then present himself as the only person who can help the victim out of this contrived predicament. The sociopath may claim that he is protecting his coworker (e.g., "He was going to go get a job somewhere else and steal me away"), or that he has sacrificed in some exceptional way for his boss. Cultivating a sense of indebtedness allows him to use the normal human regard for reciprocity to manipulate the victim into doing favors for him. Often, the favors the sociopath asks are risky or unethical or otherwise uncomfortable for the targeted person (e.g., "Let me take a peek at the boss's books").

5. *Hiring yes-men.* An employer who is sociopathic may preferentially promote or hire someone he predicts will easily be made to feel real or imaginary indebtedness, giving no concern whatsoever as to that person's qualifications for the job. Feeling beholden, such an employee can be irrationally loyal and will tend to help buffer the sociopathic boss from discovery by others both outside and inside the organization. This tactic sometimes speaks to the baffled questions of other employees wondering why a seemingly intelligent boss—who, unbeknownst to them, is a sociopath—has

promoted or hired an obviously incompetent or repellent person. Even if this hyper-devoted employee catches on to the true nature of his sociopathic boss, in all probability he himself will be too implicated in unethical or frankly illegal schemes to be inclined to blow the whistle.

WHAT NOW? A GUIDE FOR PROTECTING YOURSELF AGAINST A SOCIOPATH AT WORK

The stress of being targeted by a workplace sociopath is dangerous to both your mental and your physical health. Your goal (the "win") is to end the torment, so that you can go back to the life you knew before—a healthy, normal life that included doing your work and feeling safe *simultaneously.*

Whether you have been targeted by a sociopathic boss or a sociopathic coworker, here are steps you can take to make the suffering stop:

1. MAINTAIN EMOTIONAL PRIVACY

In a workplace, allowing the sociopath who has targeted you to view your anger, fear, and confusion is like pouring sugar onto yeast. The sociopath will feed on your distress, and his shameless manipulations will multiply. He wants to have "power" over you—to make you jump and to witness your exposed emotions. Maintain your emotional privacy, so that you do not reward his behavior with exactly what he wants to see.

Remain calm—or, if you cannot, then aim for the appearance of calm—but if the sociopath approaches you directly, you do not need to pretend that you are simply oblivious. Though certainly not a requirement, it is fine to acknowledge, in a matter-of-fact manner, that you know about the sociopath's actions. If you wish to let the sociopath know that you are on to him, then briefly and neutrally state that you are aware of what he or she has done and are concerned about the negative effects of these actions on the company's productivity. In this way, you place the sociopath on notice that you will not be made to jump and that you view his or her behavior as *an impediment to the work goals of the group*.

Resist the temptation to announce what you are going to do about the situation. *Serene silence about your intentions can be incredibly powerful when you are speaking with someone who is trying to control you.* If he or she directly asks what you intend to do, you can say calmly, "I haven't decided yet." If he or she does not want to accept this answer, give the very same emotionless answer again (three or four times, if he or she continues to press you): "I haven't decided yet." This, by the way, will be a truthful statement.

Try to be the one who ends any conversation with the sociopath. Tell him or her that you have to go, and then walk away—calmly. If he or she tries to stop you or angrily follows you, so much the better, especially if other people are present to witness it.

Remaining calm will assist you in carrying out steps 2 and 3 as well, and in showing others in the workplace that you are a composed and rational person who does not become "hysterical" under stress.

2. DECIDE

Do you genuinely want to stay in this job and fight, or is your true fantasy to stand up, someday very soon, and simply walk out of a job that is damaging your life? This is a valid question, and you must be honest with yourself when you answer. Convincing a company that it should confront your sociopathic boss or co-worker can be an extremely frustrating endeavor. Workplaces strongly resist change, especially change that involves conflict. In their attempts to avoid change, even normal, essentially well-meaning people will sometimes blame the messenger—you—because you are the one insisting that they recognize and deal with a strange, unsettling, and perhaps even frightening situation. I urge you to consider this difficult truth before you decide what to do. Fortunately, you have options in how you will deal with being targeted by a sociopath, and getting the sociopath ousted—singlehandedly rectifying an entire organization—is only one possible course of action. Another reasonable choice is to leave this job relatively soon and on your own terms, with the legitimate goal of taking responsible care of yourself and the people who love you.

3. ACT

If your decision is to try to convince the company to deal with the sociopath, proceed with these steps:

Keep thorough records. Begin by documenting the sociopath's duplicity and treachery at work. List *each significant lie* he or she tells—to you or anyone, about anything that is work-related—as soon as you become aware of it. Do not wait until the next day or the weekend to do this; you should record each event you experience or hear about while it is fresh in your mind. For each entry, note the date and write a brief description of what happened. Include the consequences of the lie, if you have knowledge of them. List *each instance of deceitful and damaging behavior* as well. If the sociopath takes credit for your work or someone else's, record that. If he or she viciously insults or embarrasses you or someone else, list and date that. If he or she deletes some of your emails or steals memos, leaving you uninformed of a new company policy or an important meeting, record the activity. If he or she intentionally sabotages your contribution to a team project, add that incident to the list.

Be unemotional and concise in your record-keeping. One very effective approach is to organize your information as an uncluttered chart that has three columns: DATE, EVENT, and CONSEQUENCES (if known). Number each entry and, *in a separate file,* record the names of the people who were present during each incident, for possible use should your complaint become a court case later on. You will *not* want to share the names during an in-house meeting, since these individuals have not yet agreed to serve as witnesses, and suddenly pulling them into the fray may severely alienate people who otherwise might have been your allies.

In your absence, a sociopath who has targeted you will almost certainly try to look through your possessions. When you leave work each day, take your documentation home with you. In addition, strengthen and update your computer passwords and remove from your workspace all non-work papers (personal letters, bank statements, bills, etc.). Sociopaths are masterful at using other people's seemingly innocuous personal information against them.

Do not be concerned right now about providing court-worthy proof. *The purpose of your initial documentation is to help you conceptualize the sociopath's activities as a threat to the bottom line of the company.* With your organized record-keeping, you may be able to demonstrate that this person's dishonest and uncooperative behavior prevents projects from being completed on time, or sometimes at all, and reduces the overall quality of the company's work. Your objective will be to help higher management understand that having this deceitful and manipulative person in the workplace is simply too expensive.

Do not take your information to the human resources (HR) department. The primary goal of HR is not to assist individual employees. Rather, the department is there to help the company's executives hire, deal with, and stabilize personnel. An HR official may not be against you, but he will not be for you, either. He is extremely unlikely to help you create change in the organization, not even constructive change. To the contrary, with the goal of keeping the company and its executives clear of conflict and potential legal difficulties, he will try to smooth the waters that you are stirring up.

The sociopath's immediate supervisor should be avoided as well. This person was likely involved in hiring the sociopath in the first place, and if so will be worried about exposing that unfortunate decision to criticism. Also, a person who is close to the sociopath in the organizational structure may have been charmed by him or her, seduced, or even blackmailed.

4. AIM HIGH

Schedule an appointment with someone closer to the top of the organization. In ordinary circumstances, bypassing human resources and going over the head of the supervisor or the boss (and perhaps the boss's boss) would be considered inappropriate, but this is no ordinary circumstance. Here, you are dealing with a sociopath, who has more than likely surrounded himself with people who will not or cannot challenge him. If you follow protocol and go to someone in the human resources department or to an immediate supervisor in your own department, it is more than possible that you will be dealing with an individual who has been completely charmed by the sociopath or perhaps beguiled into taking risks, sexual or otherwise, that have left the official or the supervisor vulnerable to extreme embarrassment and the possibility of losing his or her job.

Do not tell anyone at work that you are making this appointment, as gossip is nearly unavoidable and you do not want your plans to be shared with the sociopath.

Prepare and rehearse an organized presentation so that, at the meeting with the person you have chosen, you can *show and explain your documentation succinctly*, in fifteen to thirty minutes. Before you leave the meeting, make certain to recommend interventions the company might make—monitoring this extremely problematic individual, demoting, or, optimally, dismissing him—for the sake of the company's financial bottom line. Tell the truth: this person is too expensive for the company to keep. You have to speak up or the bosses will try to keep the peace instead of going after the sociopath.

Be composed and businesslike at this meeting. You are not there to ask a favor for yourself. You are there to provide important information about a costly problem within the organization and to offer possible solutions. Do not express your emotions or any sense that you have been victimized. Sadly, people who represent themselves as victims are often perceived as weak, and advice from them is seldom taken seriously. Speak with calm objectivity rather than as someone who has been injured.

Do not use the word *sociopathic* or any other diagnostic or psychological term. Instead, use the kind of direct, common-sense words that people understand right away: *lies, undercuts, insults, tricks, manipulates, steals,* and so forth, and keep the discussion centered on his or her destructive dishonesty. It is not important to convince an executive manager that the person under discussion has a personality disorder. Insisting on this point can sidetrack the discussion and subvert your true objective, which is to get something done about the unacceptable situation in the company.

5. EVALUATE THE ORGANIZATION'S RESPONSE

If, within a reasonable period of time, the company asks you for more information and investigates what you have reported, or actively proceeds to monitor, demote, or dismiss the sociopath, you deserve to congratulate yourself on this hard-won achievement. Since the company has acted, you can stay at your current job, if you still wish to do so. If, on the other hand, the company does nothing, leaving you to deal with the sociopath on your own, you will need to decide whether or not this unresponsive organization is one in which you want to invest forty or more hours per week of your life.

To scuttle the plans of the sociopath who is being harbored by this company, you may need to leave. The assistance of a lawyer will be helpful at this point. A lawyer can work with the fact that, though you have informed the company of a serious and potentially health-damaging problem, the company has done nothing. If the cost of legal counsel is an issue, as it often is, ask your lawyer simply to write a letter, informing the company that you will consider not pursuing legal action if you are provided with a positive letter of recommendation for new employment somewhere else. Depending on the nature of your job, you may wish to ask for severance pay. Carefully think through how much money you will need to cover your expenses during a job search.

The lawyer may or may not be familiar with the technical definition of *sociopath*, but to fulfill your request, he does not need to be. Here again, you can use commonsense, nonclinical language when describing the sociopath's behavior and its effects on you and others. Understand that your lawyer will be much more interested in the company's irresponsible failure to correct a harmful situation than in a psychological analysis of the sociopath.

The sociopath now likely believes he has cornered you inside a negligent company. He is entertained by the thought of your distress, and feels confident in his ability to control you. *But the truth is that he is not in control of you, and you are not trapped.* By leaving on your own terms, you can preserve your emotional privacy, maintain control, and take positive action to return peace to your life.

If you are in a partnership or a very small company—in other words, if there is no senior management in the usual sense—you may well have to take the sociopath to court. Deceitful behavior that causes loss is legally actionable. The same is true if you are being publicly slandered, regardless of the size or nature of your workplace. In the event of slander, the loss may include your good name and the value of your work, which are both arguably more important than any particular job. Going to court is expensive in terms of both money and time, but in these cases— being targeted by a partner, or by someone within a small company, or seeing your work or yourself publicly smeared— taking legal action against the conscienceless individual is likely to be worth the cost. With the help of a skillful lawyer, you can disentangle yourself from the sociopath and avoid the future life-altering damage he or she may create if you do not act.

SOCIOPATHIC PROFESSIONALS

Some conscienceless people manage to slip into a deluxe cloak of invisibility that is even more effective than usual: an honored professional title or some other highly respected role in the community. There are certain professional roles that automatically cause us to view the people who occupy them as especially caring, responsible, and honorable: teacher, doctor, clergyman, and therapist, to name a few. Our expectations are met a large part of the time; thankfully, most of the doctors, teachers, and other professionals we encounter do possess integrity and compassion. These same decent and caring people are typically the most shocked and angered of all when cases of predatory professionals are discovered. When our expectations are completely defied and a trusted professional turns out to be fundamentally deceitful, the results can be unsettling, even tragic.

Since we live in a world where this is all too possible, there are two crucial truths that you should remember. First, we have a strong tendency to attribute individuals with the respectability and trustworthiness we associate with their roles and titles. In other words, we are apt to confuse people with their positions. We are inclined to forget that Dr. Mary Smith is simply a human being named Mary Smith who has a professional title before her name, and that Mary Smith herself may or may not possess the positive characteristics linked in our minds with the label "Doctor." Labels are a form of shorthand: they convey a great deal of information quickly and almost subliminally. For this reason, sometimes they efficiently assist us in our dealings with other people; but sometimes they serve only to short-circuit our vigilance. Of course, the same goes for other titles—Professor, Father, Rabbi, Reverend—and for honored roles that do not necessarily carry specific prefixes, such as teacher and parent. Titles and roles mean more or less the same thing, but the human beings who hold them should be evaluated as who they are, rather than as sure bets. You would not unquestioningly swallow a foul-smelling green liquid simply because its label read MILK.

The second key fact to remember is that certain of the professions have two attributes that are extremely and specifically attractive to sociopaths. To be a teacher, a doctor, a clergyman, or a psychotherapist is to have *interpersonal power* over a number of people who will seldom question you, and also *privacy* in the form of a professional setting that is effectively closed to outside observers (another type of "closed system"). This perspective on closed professional settings—schools, medical offices, places of worship, and session rooms—is grim, but must be considered. Psychologists have long known that unequal power plus isolation is an all-purpose formula for abuse, and any profession or vocation that includes these two elements will draw more than its fair share of sociopaths.

By far, most of the stories about ruthless professionals that I receive concern either educators or physicians, two professional groups that nearly always offer a generous measure of privacy and power within a defined setting. If you have ever been victimized by a sociopathic professional, the following letter is likely to help you feel less alone in your experience:

> *Thinking about what happened to my father sends a shiver down my spine and makes me cry. I'm sure he was murdered. He was seventy at the time. He'd had chronic lung problems for years, then he had a pulmonary embolism. After a few days in the ICU, his pulmonologist said he was doing well. When he died suddenly, we were shocked. The doctor told us that he had been weakened by the embolism and his lungs had given out. But he was very fuzzy about the details. Since my dad had seemed okay just days before, we asked for an autopsy. We found out that the doctor had not requested one. Why wouldn't he? We suspected that he knew he did something wrong and refused to*

accept responsibility. We had never liked the doctor, and had even told him that we might want another physician. When my father died soon after, we couldn't help but be suspicious. Could his ego have been more important than giving my father the right care?

We are going to send a complaint to the medical licensing board. I hope he loses his license. It's too late to help my poor father, but maybe it will save someone else's life.

Another example is a murder that stunned the city of Tucson, Arizona, in 2004. In this case, a physician named Bradley Schwartz hired someone to murder a beloved pediatric ophthalmologist, Dr. Brian Stidham.

When Stidham joined Schwartz's medical practice in 2001, he was unaware that his partner was under investigation by the DEA. Eventually, a grand jury issued a seventy-seven-count indictment against Schwartz, on charges that he had written Vicodin and Ritalin prescriptions for his lover and his office manager, who would turn these drugs over to him for his own use. Schwartz's medical license was revoked in 2002, and he was ordered into drug rehab. Dr. Stidham then went into business alone, and many patients from their shared practice went with him.

Schwartz was able to regain his medical license after rehab, but he harbored resentment against Stidham for striking out on his own. Several of Schwartz's former girlfriends (he cheated prolifically on his wife) revealed that he had talked to them about planting child pornography on Stidham's computer and throwing acid at him. He ultimately hired a former patient to kill Stidham; the killer stabbed and beat Stidham to death and tried to make it look like a robbery. Both Schwartz and the murderer were apprehended and convicted.

In an ironic twist, in prison this former ophthalmologist suffered two broken eye sockets when he was assaulted by other inmates. He would become angry when prison staff didn't address him as "Dr. Schwartz," even though his medical license had been revoked for good. He appeared to have little remorse for what he did, and even tried to sue the state of Arizona for not protecting him against harm by other inmates (he was assaulted multiple times).

People were so shocked by the discovery that a physician had arranged the murder of another physician that the story was aired in the United States by national television shows such as *Court TV* and *48 Hours,* and the reporter who covered the case for the *Tucson Citizen,* A. J. Flick, even wrote a book about it. Five years after it happened, the story of the murderous Dr. Bradley Schwartz made it all the way from Arizona to the United Kingdom, where it was chronicled once again, on the Discovery Channel.

Even a cursory look at Schwartz's personal history should have raised the strong suspicion that he was a sociopath—if anyone had thought to check behind the title of "Dr." His story was that of a man with a lifelong involvement in coldly calculated sexual liaisons, fraud, drug abuse, and domestic violence. He was sexually involved with the foster mother of one of his patients, who allowed him to use her name to acquire prescriptions for hydrocodone. The domestic violence between Schwartz and his lover was so extreme and repeated that, in 2003, one year before the murder of his colleague, Schwartz was placed on a five-year probation by the Arizona Medical Board, for "unprofessional conduct." The antisocial pattern was there all along, but no one had ever noticed it. It had been hiding behind a title nearly all of us respect automatically: Doctor.

I am particularly bothered by accounts concerning educators, like this one:

> What has happened to my son recently made me think of your book. Mark has had to deal with severe depression and anxiety from a young age. He's in college now, and last semester he was talking about suicide a lot. We thought he should take a year off, but he said he was ready to go back.
>
> Mark was majoring in Russian literature and was really looking forward to meeting the professor who was teaching one of his courses that fall. The professor, who was highly regarded, also became my son's adviser. My son was seeing one of the school psychologists on a regular basis at the time. Somehow the professor found out about it. From that point on, his communications with my son took a bad turn. He would often ridicule my son. It shattered Mark's confidence and gave him episodes of severe anxiety. He became afraid to even look at this man, and his grade in this professor's class plummeted.
>
> I finally requested a meeting with the professor. It was a very disturbing encounter. At first, he feigned ignorance about any problems. Then he chastised us both for daring to accuse him of inappropriate behavior. From there, he went full circle. By the end of the meeting, he seemed almost apologetic about the concerns my son had.
>
> My son managed to pass the class and did well in his other courses. He requested a new adviser and realized that he could

complete his major without having this professor again. But I can feel myself going into a rage when I think about this professor being allowed to stay in his position at the school. Who knows how many students he has intimidated, and will continue to?

WHAT NOW? PROTECTING YOURSELF AGAINST A SOCIOPATHIC PROFESSIONAL

Being targeted by heartlessly controlling and remorseless professionals is crazy-making. In such cases, we are harmed by the very people who are supposed to be helping us. Even if we find a way to put a stop to this in our own situation, we often feel guilty and somehow responsible for the future victimization we are nearly certain will occur somewhere else. Long after our own ordeal is over, we can remain frustrated and angry that, over and over again, such individuals seem to get away with their devastating under-the-radar activities.

Against what seems to be popular belief, a malpractice case in court is very difficult to win. The complainant must prove that the damage was life-threatening and/or permanent, and the standard of proof is exceedingly high. Often, even physical injuries do not meet the qualifications for professional malpractice, and purely psychological wounds almost never do. A far better course of action is to register a complaint with the individual's licensing board. Losing a professional license—or being discovered as practicing without one—is no small limitation, even for a sociopath. A licensing board is serious about its task (preserving the integrity and reputation of its profession), and a case before the board often does not require the same standard of proof to suspend and sometimes revoke a license. Complaining to the sociopath's professional licensing board has the further advantage to you of being less expensive than a court case would be.

Call the relevant licensing board for your state and request information about how to file a complaint. In most cases, the process will begin with a letter from you, not very different from the letters in this chapter, along with whatever evidence you can gather. Frequently, complainants will hire a lawyer to help them compose this letter, assist with any in-person testimony they need to make, and question the offender. Once again, even with the professionals on the board, you will want to avoid the counterproductive distraction of insisting on a diagnosis of sociopathy. I recommend working with a lawyer who has a general specialty or subspecialty in licensing board complaints.

If you "win"—if the board decides there is enough merit in your complaint to suspend or revoke the sociopath's license—you will not be awarded money, and a licensing board cannot impose the same punishment on the offender that a court might. But you probably will protect another person, and perhaps several people, from having to endure the same heartless games of a sociopath that you did. You will have won your own battle in the crucial struggle between human caring and sociopathy.

Sociopaths wield a powerfully destructive influence on us as individuals, families, employees, and communities—and, as we are about to see, they even abuse our time-honored legal system.

FOUR

THE SOCIOPATH IN COURT

Fighting for Child Custody

"You can fool too many of the people too much
of the time."

—JAMES THURBER

The young court-appointed counselor sat behind the desk in her new courthouse office and steeled herself for this interview with a man who had been accused of physically abusing his seven-year-old daughter. One of her clinical instructors had once remarked that, in interviews, abusers tended to be either very angry or strangely composed, but this person appeared to be neither. Instead, his body language said he was sad and possibly depressed. As he had walked in, he had not even made eye contact.

"Do you understand why we're here today, Perry?" she asked.

"I think so," he said. "My wife . . . I mean my ex-wife . . . is trying to take away my joint custody, and she's saying all kinds of things about me. And I want some time with my little Ashley, so now I guess I have to prove I'm not crazy. You're the one who's testing me, right?"

"Well, no one's trying to say that you're crazy, but some fairly serious allegations have been made about your behavior where your daughter is concerned, and the judge wants to find out a little more about you. I'm not going to test you, exactly. I'm just going to be talking with you."

"How can I prove to you that I love my little Ashley? I'd cut my own hands off before I ever hurt her! I would never, never do those horrible things Lynn says, but how am I supposed to prove it? I have to get people to listen. I *have* to, because Ashley . . . my Ashley really *needs* me."

Perry gripped the arms of his chair and stared down at the floor.

"How so? How does Ashley need you?"

Reluctantly, he looked up and said, "You won't believe me. No one will. Lynn's the mother, and no one's going to believe that a mother would . . ."

He stopped.

"If there's something the judge needs to know, you should tell me."

"If I do, you really will think I'm crazy. Even my friends think I'm crazy when I try to talk about this."

"I think you should tell me anyway. You say you care about your daughter, Perry, so if it's important for her well-being, you need to tell me. The judge will want to know."

"I guess it's the right thing to do—telling you—but it just sounds so crazy. I know you won't believe me."

"Try me."

"Lynn lies and makes up all this stuff about me being mean to Ashley and hitting her and all those awful, awful things, and meanwhile it's Lynn . . . Lynn touches Ashley. What I mean is— she touches her in ways that aren't . . . that aren't appropriate. And she lies! You can't imagine how much she lies, and everyone's going to believe her because she's the mother and I'm just the father, and if you take me out of Ashley's life . . ."

He stopped and looked down at the floor again. After a moment he said, "I'm the only protection Ashley's got. If you take me out of her life, she's completely defenseless. Please, you can't do this."

"You know that I've already spoken with Ashley, don't you, Perry?"

"Yes. Yes, I do. What did she say?"

"Well, I should tell you that Ashley said she was frightened of you."

"Frightened of *me*? Oh my God, this is a nightmare! Don't you see what this is? She's saying what Lynn told her to say. She's so scared of Lynn she's afraid to say anything else. My wife is turning my own child against me! Can't you see that? Poor little Ashley—she's only seven. She's no match for all this . . . for all this lying and manipulating. And she's not about to tell you about Lynn touching her, either. She knows Lynn would kill her. She didn't tell you about her mother, did she? No. How could you expect her to say anything?"

The counselor was taken aback, though she tried not to register surprise in her face. The father's unexpected claim about the mother certainly created complications in assessing this case for the court. Was he telling the truth? Had this mother indeed made false allegations about the father to mask her own abuse of her child? That would take a particularly alarming variety of cold-bloodedness, and it seemed so unlikely.

"These are very serious claims, Perry," she said.

"I knew you wouldn't believe me. Why would you? No one else does. But it doesn't matter what anyone thinks, I won't abandon Ashley. I close my eyes and I can see her beautiful little face, and I know I can't abandon her to that . . . to that sick woman. My wife lies as easily as she breathes. She's so good at it she's spooky. But I'll fight for my daughter. I want Ashley to know that she's . . . that she's not alone."

He looked directly at the counselor now, and his eyes filled with tears.

The conversation went on this way for another forty-five minutes, and Perry observed that the more he talked about his daughter, and the more he cried, the more accepting the counselor became of the idea that his ex-wife might be the real abuser. He had thought the counselor might give him some kind of psychological test, but she did not. After he left her office, he congratulated himself on a job well done. Acting depressed and constantly staring at the floor like that had been a nice touch.

In reality, Lynn was an especially good mother. Ashley was her life, and Lynn would protect her with her last ounce of strength— and her last dollar. He could picture the look of amazement and terror on Lynn's face when she found out he had accused her of sexually abusing Ashley, which was a particularly pleasing thought. The idea that someone might believe such a thing about her would be the worst thing Lynn could imagine. If the counselor fell for it, maybe the court would even say that Lynn's time with Ashley needed to be supervised. That would be unbearable for a mother like her. He did not really want to have the kid at his place half the time, but it would be worth the annoyance to see Lynn squirm. After a while, he would get tired of the kid and give her back—until Lynn eventually found a serious boyfriend, at which time his deep concern about her pedophilia would suddenly reemerge.

The more he pondered the custody proceedings, the more he thought he had not had this much fun since, as an eleven-year-old, he had hog-tied his mother's basset hound. He had roped all four of its stubby little legs together to watch it struggle. The thing had howled like there was no tomorrow and had thrashed around so hard that it ended up with bloody rope marks on its legs. What a blast that had been, to be able to make that stupid-looking animal do something so ridiculous. His mother had never suspected him. She believed he loved the dog.

It was stupid of Lynn to think she could beat him at this game.

SOCIOPATHY AND CUSTODY DECISIONS

Do sociopaths make bad parents?

Asking this question seems ridiculous. Anyone who knows even a little about the irresponsibility, lovelessness, and cruelty of a sociopath like Perry could answer it without thinking twice. And yet, strangely, our society tends to function as if conscience-less people make perfectly fine parents. People assume that "sociopath" is just another epithet that bitter ex-spouses toss around, much like "jerk" or "creep." Our society and our legal system regard those who insist on raising the question as if they were merely bothersome and, in many cases, crazy.

I receive many letters on this subject from the grown children of sociopathic parents, and, as one might surmise, all of these letters answer the question I posed—*Do sociopaths make bad parents?*—with a resounding *Yes, they do.* Sociopaths tend to shatter the lives of the children who are directly under their control, and the damage can last long into adulthood.

> *My father just doesn't have a conscience. It took me a long time to understand this. I'm 29, long removed from his clutches, but I'm still suffering. My parents divorced when I was little. Joint custody meant that I had to go to my father's house on alternate weekends. For five years, he sexually abused me. When I started high school, I just left his house one day and never went back.*
>
> *I still find it hard to trust anyone. I have depression and I get anxiety attacks. I am haunted every day by one question: What would I be like today if someone had stopped him from doing that to me? Why do we allow people like him to be around kids at all?*

Indeed, why do we let them? Part of the answer is that, as I have described, the remorseless are good at looking like everyone else—at being effectively invisible—and at keeping even their most egregious activities off the legal and social radar. Another partial answer is that sociopaths often focus their attentions on the "easy marks," the defenseless and the voiceless. And who could be an easier mark than one's own young children?

But something more is going on here. The natural skill set of the sociopath empowers him only to a certain degree. The rest of his power comes from us, as a society. Like the counselor who interviewed Perry, we sincerely want to protect the innocent, most especially children, but too much of the time we unwittingly protect their tormenters instead. As a society, we want to do the right thing, but thanks to misperceptions and outdated procedures where the conscienceless are involved, we often bring more darkness than light.

Consider the following account of activities that I believe most of us would deem to be immoral, criminal, and just the sort of behaviors from which our legal system would take great care to protect young children. But this is not what happened. Instead, as in far too many other cases, the legal system failed both the normal (non-sociopathic) parent and the children:

> *They say that the children suffer most during a divorce, and you can multiply that when you have a husband like mine. Three years after our split, my children and I are still dealing with the damage from him.*
>
> *I met David when he was a first-year law student. I was working part-time as a waitress in a bar near his school, where he would flirt and joke with me late into the night. After we'd been dating awhile, he told me that he liked my family a lot more than his own, rich one. He said that his parents had always ignored him, going back to when he was a little child.*

David became obsessed with me, calling me all the time and wanting to be with me every night. We got married while he was still in law school, and I worked two jobs to help pay for it. He claimed his parents wouldn't contribute a cent. By the time he finished school, we had a daughter and a son.

David had been working at a local law firm when he got an offer from a firm three hours away. I didn't want to be that far from my parents. They were a great help with the kids. The relationship hadn't been going well and I asked him if he thought we still had a future together. He took me in his arms and said I would always be the only one for him. Only later I realized that he didn't mention the kids. I began to feel that his sentiment was all an act. There was no real feeling for me.

Things got worse between us and I was worried. David was away a lot on business and we hardly talked. But still we had a third child. It was a strain on me, to have responsibility for three little kids. Then a woman knocked on the door one day and told me that the new carpeting would be installed the next day. When I told her we hadn't ordered any new carpeting, she mentioned David by name and said he had requested it. She said she needed to look around the house, but she didn't measure anything or ask me to sign anything. Eventually she just nodded and left without a word. I called David about it and he told me it must have been a scam, that I should forget about it.

A year later, the same woman showed up. She brought in two giant suitcases and threw them on the living room floor before storming out. My children were having play dates with some friends at the time and were a little frightened. Then she dropped a bomb: she came back in holding a baby and said that

David was the father! He told me it was a prank by someone at his firm, a running gag. I tried to believe him. I couldn't bear to accept that my husband could do such a thing. A few weeks later I got a call from a secretary at his office who had recently left the firm. She told me that she'd often heard him talking on the phone in a lovey-dovey way to a woman with a different name than mine. That was the last straw. I knew I had to file for divorce. He got angry when I mentioned it, packed a bag, and left.

After I got a lawyer, I found out that his "business trips" had been time spent with this other woman. He had spent thousands of dollars on her. He didn't care where the money came from. One day I tried to take cash out of our joint account at the ATM and found out there was a zero balance!

I think the hardest thing I ever had to do was tell the kids that their father and I were divorcing. When I let David know I had told them, he blubbered like a baby. Then he talked to the children, and they were obviously confused. I can imagine what lies he told them. I'm sure he blamed me entirely.

David went to live with the other woman and their son. But before the divorce was finalized, he would drive around our neighborhood, sort of stalking us. I found out that he was trashing me to the neighbors, telling them that I had been cheating on him.

I thought things would settle down after the divorce, but David continually tried to turn the kids against me. It was so stressful for them. Of course, my husband had visitation rights. I couldn't stop him, because psychological abuse wasn't considered sufficient to deny contact where I lived; it had to be physical or sexual. I knew the visits were emotionally damaging for them. My 15-year-old daughter, Olivia, stopped seeing him about a year after the divorce. David fought to retain the visitation rights, but a social worker sided with Olivia. David's reaction was to see Olivia as my ally, therefore his enemy. My daughter burst into tears one day after he had harangued her on the phone.

The divorce may have been final, but the emotional stress on my children went on. At least Olivia was able to avoid exposure to him. Claire and Jason, who were 9 and 12, weren't so lucky; they were considered too young to make a judgment about the visitations, so my ex was still allowed time with them. On one occasion, he took them on a trip to the beach. I had tried to prevent it, and even Claire's therapist said it was not a good idea. David ignored the therapist's advice, but he promised me that his girlfriend and her son wouldn't be there. Of course, they both did go. My ex and his woman fondled each other on the beach, right in front of the kids. They even made the kids cook dinner while they swigged cocktails and danced around half naked on the deck of the rented cottage.

Often my children came home from visits trembling. They would almost never talk about what happened. The stress mounted and took its toll. Claire became anorexic and had to be hospitalized. Jason retreated into a nearly 24/7 world of video games.

I know that the strain of David's behavior has compromised me as a mother, but I've tried my best. It's three years after the divorce now, and Olivia is doing relatively okay. She's in college and sees the school psychologist once a week. Claire's weight keeps yo-yoing back and forth. She's seeing an eating-disorder therapist as well as a regular therapist. I'm most worried about Jason. He's up all night with his computer games, and his grades suffer. I can't seem to reach him. Except for Olivia, my kids still sometimes question why I won't try to fix things with Daddy. I know David has never stopped feeding them lies about me. He tells them how sorry he is that Mommy broke up the family, that Mommy doesn't think they deserve to have a dad. Then he puts on his repentance act with the neighbors. He says that he made a mistake and wants to make things right, but that I've unfairly rejected him.

Extraordinary as this story may seem, there are many other people in similar situations. Of the letters I have received since publishing *The Sociopath Next Door,* by far the thickest file is the one that contains stories of legal struggles. Most of these letters describe what I refer to as "sociopathic custody games," in which the ruthless have used the legal system as if it were a convenient set of tools to manipulate and control other people.

Most sociopathic custody games follow a pattern. First, the sociopathic spouse realizes that pursuing custody of the children is extremely gratifying, even though he or she cannot care about the children and probably will have no genuine wish to parent them after the thrill of winning has passed. The sociopath has the opportunity to join in legal games, which are entertaining for him because he relishes games and is good at them. The gratification is intensified when he discovers how many hoops the other parent will jump through in desperate attempts to rescue the children. Causing the spouse or ex-spouse to jump enhances the sociopath's sense of being in control, which is his central pre-occupation.

Next, the legal system that is supposed to protect the children fails to do so. The system is deceived and overwhelmed by the sociopath's gamesmanship: his barefaced lies, his no-holds-barred manipulations, and his ability to represent himself as the injured party. In addition—tragically—the system often does not understand the gravity of the risk to the children.

Last, the non-sociopathic parent is increasingly panic-stricken, as an unacceptable fate for the children appears more and more likely. The frantic behavior of this parent, who truly loves the children, becomes "hysterical" from the viewpoint of the attorneys, the court, and sometimes even friends and family, who then may decide that her "hysteria" is evidence that she is an unfit parent. The normal, loving parent is drained of personal and financial resources, and feels stupid, crazy, and alone. Nonetheless, his or her love for the children makes giving up impossible, and he or she continues to try to rescue the children, often for many years.

When the loving parent has fewer financial resources than the sociopath, the sociopath's legal manipulations can be even more devastating, as in the following example of a custody game:

> Me getting together with Michael in the first place seems a little crazy to me now. I was only nineteen when I met him, and he was in his mid-thirties. It was the summer after my freshman year in college and I was working at a day camp where his two kids went. Michael used to come pick them up and he'd always joke around with me. After a few weeks of sort of flirting with

each other, he asked me out, assuring me that it was legit: he was divorced. The age difference hit me hard and I said no, but that wouldn't do it. He had become obsessed with me. I was walking across campus that fall and he suddenly appeared in front of me as I was about go to my biology class. It seemed so romantic. He had taken a small studio apartment in town, and before long I was staying over there most nights. The honeymoon ended pretty soon, though. He demanded to know my schedule down to the minute every day and would fly into a rage if I didn't come to the apartment right after my last class. He was often high when I came back. The empty liquor bottles piled up and there was always a haze of marijuana smoke in the place.
[To put this aspect of the story in context: the American Medical Association estimates that as many as 75 percent of sociopaths are dependent on alcohol, and 50 percent abuse other drugs.]

I couldn't seem to overcome Michael's demands on my time. Studying became next to impossible, and I ended up flunking out. My parents were furious and told me that I would have to take out loans if I wanted to ever go back. I should have left him, I guess, but I thought I was in love and tried to downplay the problems to myself. And I had little financial resources of my own.

Michael was furious when the school year ended and I decided to go back home to my parents and get my life back together. He moved again, to a small place over a store in my hometown. I got a job at a local pharmacy but Michael soon found out, and he used to come in there all the time. He'd wander the aisles until finally the manager told him he was no longer welcome in the store.

Meanwhile, a pregnancy test told me what I had been fearing. I told Michael about it and it enraged him. I knew I couldn't get an abortion. I have a strong Catholic faith and couldn't even consider such an option. But I couldn't face my parents, so I moved in with Michael again. He put pressure on me to end the pregnancy, but I wasn't going to do it. I let myself think that he'd be a good father, like I'd seen him be with his other kids, and that we would get married. But the drinking got worse than ever. He would throw glasses against the wall, and slap me sometimes, really hard. Once he even knocked me down, but then he cried like a baby, thinking he might have hurt me. He seemed to be better toward me for a while after that, right up to the baby's birth. Then he refused to let my parents see the baby. When I threatened to leave, he told me that he would call the police and tell them that I was abusive to my daughter. He actually tried to file a restraining order against me. For a short time he had sole custody of my daughter because he knew how to work the law and had a lot more money to work with than I did. I was considered to not have enough resources to take care of a child. I was forced to be evaluated by a social worker, then a psychiatrist. The stress was overwhelming. I finally got my child back, but the legal system didn't make it easy for me.

My daughter is five years old now, and Michael still continues to wreak havoc. I just want to break free from him completely, but he keeps trying to force me to give up my child to him. I can't get much help from my parents because my father got disabled and can't work anymore, plus he's never forgiven me for the sin of having a child out of wedlock. I wonder sometimes if Michael acted the same way with his previous family. Maybe he tried to *steal custody of those kids, too. I'm not sure I'll ever recover from what he's done to me. I have been diagnosed with PTSD.*

This story, in which a violent abuser is granted sole custody of a minor child, should be a rare exception within our legal system, but it reflects the norm. The American Psychological Association has found that abusive parents are more likely to seek sole custody than are nonviolent ones, and the American Judges Foundation reports that about 70 percent of these abusers are successful in gaining sole custody. These statistics astonish most people—that is, people who have not faced a sociopath in court.

How is this happening? Why are we acting in a way that is diametrically opposed to the best interests of the child, and accomplishing exactly the opposite of what we intend? Part of the reason is that the "custody game" has been rigged, accidentally, in favor of the sociopath. American courts operate under the presumption that the interests of the child are best served by joint custody, and the courts will often hold this precept above the commonsense observation that some parents are simply too psychologically and physically dangerous to be granted any level of custody. While it is arguable that two involved parents are better than one when both parents possess conscience and a normal ability to love, this formula breaks down when it is applied without examining the history of both parents for abuse, domestic violence, and other antisocial behaviors.

Another easy loophole for the sociopath to exploit involves the "friendly parent doctrine," in which the parent who is deemed more likely to encourage a relationship between the child and the other parent is more likely to be awarded custody. In the angry and vengeful atmosphere that often surrounds divorce proceedings, trying to "get" the children can easily become a way for one or both parents to express anger and attempt revenge; the friendly parent doctrine was designed to keep the children of divorcing couples from becoming the spoils of a domestic war. Sadly, this doctrine has become yet another tactic used by sociopaths to make the other spouse jump, to manipulate the legal system, and to win at the "game." The sociopath alarms the other parent concerning the future of the children—making her "hysterical" and increasingly accusatory in court—while he himself remains calm (sociopathically so), thereby demonstrating his "friendliness" before the judge.

The friendly parent doctrine evolved from the court's concern about "parental alienation," the process by which one parent psychologically poisons the relationship between the child and the other parent. Unfortunately, the parental alienation concept requires the court to assume that the child's negative feelings have no basis in reality. (You may recall that, in the case described at the start of this chapter, the court-appointed counselor was coming to accept the version of reality presented by the sociopathic father, Perry, over that of his daughter, Ashley.) This assumption ignores the behaviors of the abusive parent and obscures the simple fact that the abuser may have poisoned the child's feelings himself, by being intimidating, humiliating, and in many cases violent toward the other parent and the understandably alienated child.

On the whole, whenever the courts have tried to fashion a modern-day King Solomon's sword—a guiding principle to help them make wise custody decisions—sociopaths have wrested away the blade and used it to torment and control loving parents. Fortunately, the joint custody "solution," the parental alienation concept, and the friendly parent doctrine are relatively new ideas; eventually, they may be modified or simply retired.

Modern custody law has already gone through a number of twists and changes. By the middle of the twentieth century, a judicial trend preferring mothers in custody disputes was well established in case law and had been codified by many state legislatures. Then, beginning in the 1970s, a major shift occurred, and most states adopted different laws, giving equal custodial status to mothers and fathers and introducing a preference for joint custody that has lasted to the present day. At the same time, the courts began to assume an active role in monitoring parental behavior. Toward the end of the twentieth century, overwhelmed by the steadily increasing number of divorce cases before them, and with no knowledge-based decision rules to decide child custody when it was disputed, judges began to look to behavioral scientists and mental health professionals to provide guidance. In the twenty-first century, the involvement of scientists and clinicians is still a relatively new practice, and the amount of influence such nonlegal experts should be allowed to have in the courtroom is a hotly debated issue. Also, it remains to be seen whether or not mental health professionals will provide tools and guidelines for custody decisions that are not simply appropriated by the ruthless, as existing guidelines have been.

EDUCATE YOUR LAWYER

Our legal system was developed to address the concept of justice and the issues of law and lawbreaking. It was not designed to confront sociopathy, which rolls its eyes at the notion of even-handedness and does not so much break the rules as it bends, tunnels under, and subverts them, with "extra points" for cleverly abusing the legal system. At its best, our system takes on complex matters of right and wrong, while sociopathy concerns itself only with winning versus losing.

Seven interrelated aspects of our legal system tend to give sociopaths a leg up in custody decisions and most other domains of the law:

1. At the outset of any proceeding, our legal system relies on the notion that people will not lie under oath, at least not without significant anxiety—but deceit delivered in an attitude of icy calm is a hallmark of sociopathy.

2. Our legal system attempts to separate the guilty from the innocent *in terms of the laws of the land,* but, as we have seen, intelligent sociopaths often learn how to manipulate situations and torment people without fully breaking those laws, or at least without leaving any admissible evidence that they have. They work under the radar. The resulting limitation in the system highlights the difference between prosecuting the lawbreaker and prosecuting the "moral criminal," who violates "only" moral directives and human decency.

3. The legal system can be viewed and successfully approached as a game, most especially by someone who lives only to win games and whose sole interest in other people is their usefulness as game pieces. But there is no regulation in place to monitor or even identify such behavior.

4. The relationship of the law to mental illness introduces the risk that, at the end of the day, a diagnosis of sociopathy might be more beneficial to the criminal than to society. As the leading example of this risk—might an insanity plea, submitted to avoid imprisonment, eventually be constructed from the sociopath's "mental illness," his very absence of conscience? In short, might the diagnosis be used in court as an argument to mitigate sentences? Because of the recent advances in our knowledge of how sociopathic brains differ from normal ones, legal experts and psychologists are already beginning to wonder. Psychologist Adrian Raine of the University of Pennsylvania phrases the question this way: "If psychopaths lack a core moral sense, as observed by reduced activation in [brain] areas important in moral decision-making, are they to blame for their actions?" (Developments in neuroscience that are relevant to ethics and the law have given rise to a new discipline called "neuroethics," but this hybrid field is still too new to provide a clear legal answer to Dr. Raine's portentous question.)

5. Our judicial system relies heavily on the concepts of repentance and rehabilitation—and sociopaths, by definition, are not repentant, nor can they ever be truly rehabilitated. Reconciling the basic nature of the sociopath with the current legal reasoning behind the use of punishment is probably impossible.

6. The system prides itself on its ability to be objective. The court's view of a person's character, good or bad, can never alter the "facts" or the pattern of "facts," which

theoretically constitute the system's only valid concern. The system took its shape when the human population was far less overwhelming, and the requirement of "complete objectivity" was mitigated by our living in smaller communities, where everyone, including the legal counselors and the judge, tended to be acquainted with everyone else, along with his or her personal history. Antisocial traits were more difficult to conceal. Today, in an overcrowded world, information about character can be largely unknown and successfully evaded. But eschewing information about character does not enhance objectivity so much as it enables a poorly informed decision, and in a custody dispute a decision that is insufficiently informed can place a child in active danger.

7. As related to the above, the contemporary legal system can be said to operate according to what many developmental psychologists call the "conventional level of moral development," in which adherence to rules and conventions is rigid, and a rule's appropriateness or fairness is not questioned. At this unevolved psychological level, the complex question of moral versus immoral behavior is seen as merely a matter of following or breaking the established rules. Or the system itself may be viewed as simply sociopathic, in the sense that it values the rules—the "game"—over people, and holds that, as long as the game is served and protected, the other, more human outcomes are not its concern. Seen in either light—the cynical or the somewhat less so—our legal system offers an uneven playing field that well suits the sociopath's gaming skills.

Many people ask me how to go about proving to the court, and even to their own attorneys, that an opponent is sociopathic. Also, I am frequently asked for referrals to attorneys who "specialize" in dealing with sociopaths. By far the most helpful advice I can give is this: *Do not try to prove that your spouse is sociopathic.* The desire to do so is completely understandable, but it will not serve you well. The courts are not currently interested in this diagnosis, and pursuing proof of it will usually lead to your being gaslighted and defeated by the sociopath. Even when the sociopathic tendencies of a parent are evaluated by an outside professional, the court will be largely uninformed about and unresponsive to the diagnosis, preferring to deal instead with the parent's specific behaviors and the proven effects of these on the child. A psychiatric diagnosis—*any* psychiatric diagnosis—is simply too easy to spin, obfuscate, and refute in a courtroom. Correspondingly, attorneys who "specialize" in sociopathy are nearly nonexistent.

Instead, focus your energies on keeping a record of the abusive and violent *behaviors and incidents* you observe or that have been reported. Most useful of all are police records of domestic violence, when such documentation exists. Because these records may be crucial to your success in court—and because knowing that you have collected evidence of the truth will most likely enrage the sociopath and possibly inspire him to attempt theft—keep them in a small safe or a secure lockbox in your home, and do not reveal their location to anyone but your lawyer.

In court, and also when speaking with your attorney, use words that are universally understood, such as *abusive, deceitful, manipulative, violent,* and *cruel,* rather than *sociopathic.* Include records of the bullying, coercion, and violence done to *you* as well as your children.

Be sure to discuss the following research summary with your attorney to acquaint her or him with the very real risks you and your children are facing. In this summary, the word *sociopath* does not occur. You will find that your attorney and the court are much more interested in plain-language descriptions of behaviors that have been shown scientifically to have harmful effects on children. Mental health professionals, legal professionals, and many nonprofessionals as well understand that violence committed against a child constitutes child abuse and is psychologically disastrous, but almost no one is aware that *merely living with an assaultive parent causes psychological damage to a child.* To help yourself in a legal struggle, you must acquaint your attorney with the relevant research. Do not assume that she or he already has this information.

RESEARCH SUMMARY OF THE EFFECTS OF SPOUSAL VIOLENCE ON CHILDREN

In 2002, Peter Jaffe, Nancy Lemon, and Samantha Poisson, authors of the field's founding text, *Child Custody & Domestic Violence,* explained, "Historically, children were viewed as unscathed if they *themselves* were not directly abused. However, growing research in this area has demonstrated the very opposite to be true. Researchers . . . have identified a host of behavioral, emotional, and psychological difficulties associated with exposure to domestic violence. In general, this research suggests that exposure to parental violence is a form of psychological abuse and can be harmful to children *both in the short term and over their life span.*"

Prominent developmental psychologists Penelope Trickett and Cynthia Schellenbach have provided a review of twenty-four separate studies of the effects on children of exposure to marital violence. All twenty-four found that *children who witnessed spousal violence had serious psychological debilities that children who were not exposed to this type of violence did not have.* Gayla Margolin, a recognized expert in this area, states that, from the unusually consistent results of these many studies, "one may conclude that witnessing violence between one's own parents is a particularly insidious event."

Research has found that a spouse batterer will assault his or her partner an average of three times a year, and that a change for the better should not be assumed simply because there has been a recent lull in the violence. Moreover, *domestic batterers tend to carry their violent behavior from relationship to relationship.* In *Child Custody & Domestic Violence,* Jaffe, Lemon, and Poisson report that 58 percent of the spouse batterers who had been studied were violent toward a new partner after the breakup of the previous relationship, and that violent spouses "may move on to new partners and continue to inflict abuse if there has been no meaningful intervention or accountability. . . . This high likelihood of continued violence results in ongoing exposure to abuse for children of divorce." These experts then add that "some judges and mental health professionals tend to view reinvolvement . . . as an indicator of stability or maturation in these new relationships," but, sadly, we now know that involvement with a new person does not indicate anything of the sort. More than half the time, in the absence of an intervention, the violence simply continues.

Worse, *more likely than not, a child in the custody of a spouse abuser will become another target for the violence.* Jaffe, Lemon, and Poisson, referring to a review of nearly three dozen separate studies on the link between spouse battering and the physical abuse of children, emphasize that all of the reviewed studies report similar empirical findings: between 30 and 60 percent of children with a parent who had been a target for violence "were themselves likely to be abused." Other reviews have found even higher statistics. In a 1998 report in the *Journal of Family Psychology,* two other noted experts, Anne Appel and George Holden, reviewed all relevant studies from the previous twenty years. They found that the percentage of overlap between spouse battering and the physical abuse of children in families was always high, in some studies reaching 100 percent. In other words, many and perhaps most spouse batterers are (or will become) child batterers as well.

Separation and divorce, rather than improving the child's circumstances, may make the batterer even more physically dangerous to the child. As Barbara Hart, a noted expert in child protective issues, has reported, "Abuse of children by a batterer is more likely when the marriage is dissolving." Hart emphasizes that, after separation and divorce, the batterer "may turn to abuse and subjugation of the children." Jaffe, Lemon, and Poisson agree. They write, "Many mental health and legal professionals naively believe that once separation has occurred, the violence is over and children's problems are historical. From our perspective, based on our experience in the justice system and knowledge of the scientific literature, this view jeopardizes the safety of . . . children. Not only is domestic violence relevant but also it should be a fundamental consideration in determining the best interest of the child postseparation."

Informed by the extensive research, many organizations have made their recommendation clear: *domestic batterers should not have sole or joint custody of minor children*. This recommendation has been endorsed by the National Council of Juvenile and Family Court Judges, which holds, "To ensure stability and permanency, children should remain in the care of their non-offending parent (or parents), whenever possible." Other organizations that endorse this policy—that the perpetrators of violence should not have either sole or joint custody of children—include the American Psychological Association and the American Bar Association. The ABA favors this presumption because (1) the batterer is ignoring the child's interests by harming the child's other parent, and (2) batterers are highly likely to use children in their care, or attempt to gain custody of their children, as a means of controlling their former spouse or partner.

And, in 1990, the U.S. Congress passed a resolution (House Congressional Resolution 172) that declared, "It is the sense of Congress that, for the purposes of determining child custody, credible evidence of physical abuse of a spouse should create a statutory presumption that it is detrimental to the child to be placed in the custody of the abusive spouse."

WHAT YOU CAN DO ON YOUR OWN, WITHOUT DEPENDING ON THE COURT

The startlingly consistent findings from research, the unambiguous policy recommendations from both the American Psychological Association and the American Bar Association, and even a congressional resolution have not yet produced a fully rational system for making child custody decisions in family court. Illustrations of this fact are sometimes astonishing. In 2009, in Dedham, Massachusetts, a twenty-year-old man named Jaime Melendez raped a fourteen-year-old girl who was alone in her home after school. As a result of the rape, the girl conceived a child. Melendez pleaded guilty to statutory rape, and a judge sentenced him to sixteen years of probation. The criminal court then referred the case to the family court, where Melendez was ordered to pay $110 a week in child support until the baby girl reached adulthood. He previously had shown no interest in the child; but, after the case went to family court, he sued for visitation, claiming that his "rights as a father" were being violated. He made it clear to the rape victim that he would drop his suit for visitation privileges if he were no longer required to pay child support. Otherwise, an unthinkable threat was implied: the young mother could anticipate having her rapist in her life—and in her daughter's life—for years. His demand for paternity rights currently drags on in the family court.

The mother's attorney, Wendy Murphy, has remarked, "You would never say to a person who suffered [any other kind of] crime, 'Sorry, we're going to let this guy further destroy your life.'" But, in fifteen states, there are no laws that explicitly deny parental rights to rapists, and without such laws a man who fathers a child through rape has the same legal rights as any other father. A rapist can petition in family court for visitation privileges or custody. Mothers have been forced to relinquish their children to visits with their rapists and to consult with their rapists over issues such as choice of school, summer camp, and religious affiliation.

Attorney Rebecca Kiessling, herself a child of rape and now an advocate for victims and their children, makes the chilling point that pursuing visitation or joint custody allows the rapist to punish the victim for testifying against him and to intimidate her so that she will take no further action. Kiessling says bluntly, "Like with rape, this is just about power and control."

The number of women and children who potentially can be controlled in this way is not small. An estimated 32,000 rape-related pregnancies occur in the United States each year, and nearly a third of pregnant victims decide to give birth to and raise their children. These numbers mean that, in the United States, approximately 10,000 women each year are vulnerable to being overpowered—again—by their rapists. In 2015, activists armed with these statistics persuaded the U.S. Congress, after years of political back-and-forth, to pass the Rape Survivor Child Custody Act. This legislation, passed by the Senate as an amendment to its human trafficking bill, provides incentives to states with laws that allow the mother of a child conceived through rape to seek court-ordered termination of the parental rights of her rapist. Qualifying states receive larger federal grants for programs authorized under the national Violence Against Women

Act (VAWA). Yet, in spite of the incentives, fifteen states still have no laws that would allow a rape victim to protect herself from the possibility that her rapist will claim the role of "co-parent"—and, worse, that her son or daughter will be made to spend time with a rapist during his or her entire childhood.

Since, in so much of the country, the law still does not prevent even a known rapist from acquiring court-sanctioned access to a child, why would we expect a family court to deny child custody to a parent who has been convicted of no legally recognized crime, simply because someone has pinned him or her with the little-understood psychological label of "sociopath"? And, since the courts have not yet reckoned with the fact that convicted rapists can use visitation and custody "rights" to manipulate and re-traumatize their victims, why should we imagine that the courts will be wiser regarding the subtler manipulative agendas of "invisibly" ruthless ex-spouses?

To improve the ability of our family court system to champion its avowed first priority (the best interest of the child), we will need to teach attorneys and judges about the child-endangering behaviors of people with certain diagnosable personality disorders; to hear less reticent, more emphatic input from psychology; and to reform family law to incorporate the consensus findings of scientific research. However, changing the fundaments of long-standing, entrenched systems takes a long time, and caring parents who are up against the ruthless are not able to wait for the psychological community to take more initiative and the family court system to change. These parents must protect themselves and their children right now.

What can you, as a loving parent, do to shield your children from a conscienceless ex-spouse who will not stop battling for the "right" to possess and use them? Since you cannot rely completely on the court as it currently functions, is there an effective lawful weapon you can use on your own?

Yes, there is. The silver bullet is both simple and powerful: *you can be boring.*

THE SILVER BULLET

There are two principal reasons that a sociopath fights for child custody. One is that he is enraged by the thought that you and the court could take away his *possessions,* which is how he thinks of you and the children. Tragically, there is nothing you can do about what he feels—and does not feel—concerning the children and you. To protect their future and yours, you will need to internalize the sad truth: the part of his brain that would allow him to love is broken.

His second and even more compelling reason to fight for custody is that, as a sociopath, he is constantly and intolerably bored. This ever-present boredom creates in him a huge need for stimulation and entertainment. *And, in this situation, you are the entertainment.* He is using the children's vulnerability to make you jump, and each time you show anger or fear, you stimulate and entertain him—and, worse, you make him feel powerful and in control.

I promise you that understanding the following counterintuitive fact is the key to your success in this struggle: the sociopath's campaign to acquire custody of the children is not primarily about the children; it is mostly about *you.* His or her focus on you means that, all on your own, you can put an end to the excitement and exhilarating sense of control a sociopath experiences during a custody battle. You can stop being infuriated, fearful, and thus entertaining for this empty person. Instead, you can be thoroughly boring.

Being boring is absolutely your best ammunition against the sociopath. If you want him or her to go away and leave you and your children in peace (which I define as the "win"), I urge you to learn about this ammunition and develop your skill at using it. Regardless of how insignificant it may sound to you as an emotionally whole person, I can assure you that, when aimed at a sociopath, this silver bullet packs a powerful punch.

Whenever he or she does something or says something to you that is frightening or enraging—in that moment, respond as if you simply do not care.

Naturally, you do care, a great deal—and when you are out of his presence, you may need to do damage control on behalf of the children and make preparations against whatever latest emergency he has concocted—but, in the moment, while he can see or hear you, act as if your emotions have not been touched at all. Rather than allowing him to see your alarm, your fear, or your anger, behave as if you are completely unconcerned.

Seeing you jump is by far the largest part of why he spends so much time and energy scheming to acquire children he does not really want to be bothered with, much less co-parent. Think of your alarm, fear, and anger as his psychological drugs. He needs these drugs badly; your job is to deprive him of his high. While he is on the phone with you, or standing before you in person, be utterly indifferent. Give unruffled, dismissive, and matter-of-fact responses. To illustrate: He comes to your door and insists he wants to come in and talk to you. You say, *"Well, I guess you can come in if you really want to. Mind if I do the dishes while we talk?"*

Then you walk casually to the kitchen and begin to wash the dishes.

He follows and tells you about something incredibly upsetting he is going to do where the children are concerned. You say, *"What's your point?"* or *"I see"*—or you reply with a distracted *"Uh-huh."*

Frustrated because he did not get the emotional reaction he anticipated, he asks whether you correctly heard what he just said. You say, *"Yes, I heard what you said. Is there anything else?"*—or *"You came here just to tell me that?"*

He doubles down on his threat and tries to make the situation sound even more menacing. But not long into his embellishment of this newest scare tactic, you announce, *"I'm getting ready to go out. Maybe we can talk some other time."*

Drying your hands, you calmly go to the door and open it for him. He is not pleased at being directed to leave, but as he tries (perhaps angrily) to keep the discussion going, you remain standing, seemingly emotionless, by the open door. Anytime you cannot think of a fitting (which is to say, totally uninterested) reply to something he says, you give him a bored-stiff sigh and wordless eye rolls.

In such a situation, you do not have to be clever, unless you want to be. Just look apathetic.

You may protest that these tactics are similar to the techniques used by the sociopath himself. But, though you are wearing a misleading mask, you are not using it to dominate and torment others, as he does. This is not a game or an addictive drug for you. Rather, you are fighting to protect the well-being of your children. Arguably, your children's future is worth your pretending for a while that you feel calmer than you really do in the face of insults and eviscerating legal threats. In the end, this quandary over the acceptable uses of guile is not strictly a psychological issue; instead it is a moral question, and I hope you will answer it for yourself in a way that allows you to shield your family from harm.

Perhaps you imagine that you are much too openly emotional to use this strategy, especially in front of someone who has known you for a long time, but please be assured that many extremely emotional people have used this approach effectively. Becoming skilled at appearing unfazed may require some work, but with preparation it is doable. Furthermore, this method sometimes succeeds even more dramatically for people who tend to respond with emotion than for those who customarily hold their feelings close to the vest, owing to the unnerving disparity between what the "audience" (in this case, your opponent in a custody case) expects of you and the indifferent response he or she now gets—an example of a potent phenomenon that psychologists refer to as a "contrast effect."

If you decide to use this "indifference method," rehearse ahead of time. Imagine possible conversations. Think of blasé replies and repeat them out loud to yourself. Practice in front of a mirror, or ask a trusted friend to role-play with you. Remind yourself of how good it will feel to preserve your privacy, to finish a discussion with a sociopath without allowing him to uncover your feelings. He is addicted to unambiguous evidence that he is able to rock your world, and you have just deprived him of his drug of choice.

Dedicate yourself to starving the sociopath's addiction to making you jump. If he directly accuses you of faking it and hiding your feelings, you do not need to argue or deny his observation. You can use the occasion to amuse yourself a little, if you wish. Maintaining your calm demeanor, you can truthfully reply, "Of course I'm being phony. Aren't you?"

You do not have to be a dazzling actor or even an especially believable one; you have only to deprive him of the emotional "payoff" you used to supply. All you need to be is bland enough to bore him, and the easiest way to accomplish this is to behave as if *he* is boring *you*. And perhaps, if you act this way long enough, you may even come to feel bored by him in reality. The game he is playing is, after all, repetitive and tedious.

Intentionally showing only bored (and boring) reactions to an adult sociopath's schemes and threats is based on the same psychological model as instituting a contingency program for a conduct disorder child (the points program described in chapter 2). Both approaches allow you to be, in a manner of speaking, a teacher who requires a disruptive "student" to learn the relationship (or the lack thereof) between certain behaviors and subsequent reward. The conduct disorder child learns that clearly specified behaviors will bring him goodies that he likes, such as sweets and action figures. In other words, the child learns that there is a link between his or her positive behaviors and what psychologists refer to as *reinforcement* (meaningful reward). Conversely, the adult sociopath learns that the goodies he once enjoyed (your overt anger, fear, and—to his way of thinking—"hysteria") do *not* follow his negative actions and verbalizations anymore. He learns that there is no longer a link between the threatening behaviors he exhibits and the reinforcement he desires.

To ensure that a certain behavior is no longer linked to reward is to place that behavior "on extinction." I can illustrate the concept of extinction with a classic animal experiment in psychology, in which a lab rat learns to press a small lever to get pellets of food. When the experimenter turns off the mechanism that delivers a food pellet to the rat each time it presses the lever, the rat will soon stop pressing. By disabling the link between lever-pressing and food, the experimenter is putting the behavior of lever-pressing on extinction.

By remaining calm—or at least giving the appearance of calm—whenever a conscienceless person harasses or threatens you, you are putting his harassing and threatening behaviors on extinction. Probably (and you need to be prepared for this) you will have to endure a few more attempts on his part, even after he appears to have given up. He may try escalating the threat or using different varieties of threat, just in case doing things a little differently might restore the former situation. Post-extinction eruptions of this kind are referred to as "extinction bursts." (Sociopaths are not usually violent in such situations, but if you face any sort of violent behavior, call the police.) Understandably, after all your hard work, his "bursts" may discourage you; but, provided they are not rewarded by visible distress on your part, these last-ditch efforts will cease and you will succeed in putting his behaviors on total extinction.

But your final goal is much more than just extinction. *You want him or her to realize that you are no fun anymore, and leave you in search of more and better psychological "drugs."* When you are completely boring, he will begin to lust for a situation he can control more easily than this vexing one with you—and without having to endure the annoyance of sharing his home with the children, an outcome he never really wanted to begin with.

He is an "emotion-eater," an addict, and his life revolves around finding a source for his next fix—someone whose strings he can pull to generate desperation and "hysteria." To rescue your children's future and your own, your job is to disconnect those strings from your emotions, so that you are no longer an easy source of entertainment and power thrills. You have little control over whether or not the court will reward his sociopathic behavior, but you have a great deal of control over whether or not *you* will reward it. By using practiced detachment and calm, you can free yourself from the sociopath's game, even when the family court fails you.

If you come to understand the game-playing patterns of the sociopath and then arm yourself with scientific research findings, you can achieve substantial success in struggles with the conscienceless, even after many years of suffering defeat. The following story was sent to me by a reader of my previous book.

A SUCCESS STORY

I am a practicing lawyer, and an adjunct professor at a prominent university. I am the furthest thing from a dummy. And yet, I fell under the thrall of a sociopath, and suffered deeply as a result.

My parents died when I was very young (7 years old). I was the oldest of five children. We were all split up to different homes, with family and close friends. I had three placements before I reached maturity. The man of the house in the family I lived with the longest was very abusive. He beat his wife (my first cousin) almost every Saturday. It was very weird—my cousins and I used to call it "Saturday night at the fights." I became very used to domestic conflict. This man also abused me physically, and was, from time to time, inappropriate with me sexually, although he did not (quite) abuse me that way. This way of dealing with men became familiar to me. School was my happy place. I was top of my class in every year, in every way. But I was so needy emotionally. I had many sexual partners. I drank ridiculous amounts as a young girl and woman. I was forever seeking validation.

After a series of intimate relationships, I finally married at the age of 29. I met my first husband in law school. He swept me off my feet. He told me I was beautiful, adorable, smart. He convinced me to do his essays for him. He passed his academic work, and the bar, with my extensive help. I did all of my own work, and at least 50% of his. He inundated me with gifts. He told me he needed to live "on the edge" all the time. This was

*very exciting to me. He had been a successful musician prior to
law school, and I am musical as well, so there was this shared (I
thought) interest in music and performance (which is always
edgy all by itself).*

*We married within six months of meeting. My professors
were all secretly horrified. They did not tell me until years later.
Now that I am a colleague, they have told me frankly what they
thought—which is that the guy was a creep, and they couldn't
understand what I was doing with him.*

*On the night before our wedding, the abuse began. He asked
me to shave myself. He insisted that I do it. He would not give
up. He got in the shower with me until I did it. I cried for
hours. Then he showered me with gifts to thank me for giving
him this "gift." And so the cycle began.*

*I gave up fabulous opportunities at big law firms in a major
city because my ex-husband did not have the same opportunities.
I ended up in a small center, in practice with him.*

*He would coerce me into mutilating myself with tattoos,
piercings, hair dye, cosmetic surgery—all in some weird attempt
to make me look like his "ideal woman." To my shame, I did it
all, because he would tell me I was beautiful afterward, and
again, he would shower me with gifts. I discovered over time
that I was paying for all of those expensive gifts, but at the time,
I did not realize the extent of his financial perfidy. He said my
job was to earn the money, and his was to "manage" it. I did all
of this because I had no self-esteem. He seemed to know this,
and took advantage of my vulnerability. I wasn't aware enough
to protect myself.*

Then the babies started coming. We had four. After each one, he would bring me home from the hospital, and I would get three or four days off. I would then have to go back to work, because he was not making any money at practicing. He said he was the "manager," and I was the worker bee. He loved me to be pregnant. It was kind of creepy. I also wanted children very much, so to some extent our needs dovetailed, but his desire to have me pregnant was sexual and disconcerting. Once the children were born, however, he was nowhere to be found. In all the time, and with all those children, he did not change ONE diaper. If I had to go out, I had to hire a baby-sitter, even if he was home. He simply could not, and would not, care for them. I earned all the money, and was the sole childcare provider.

He would disappear sometimes for a few days, and not say where he had been. He finally admitted that he was visiting prostitutes. At first I was devastated, but eventually I was relieved. The sexual demands were insane—there had to be sex on a schedule. The sex got more and more perverse as time went on, because ordinary sex was boring. A sex shop opened up in town halfway through our marriage, and it made a big splash in the paper. I was sick when I saw the article. I knew he would come home with items from this shop, and insist on trying them. He did—masks, batons, paddles, corsets, you name it. All of this was stuff way outside my own comfort zone. Again, I did it all, because he would make it inevitable. He would whine, pester, and in some cases, simply force me physically. Then he would say, "See? That wasn't so bad!" I would be in a flood of tears, or simply silent, and utterly defeated. He couldn't see any of that. If I complained, he would buy me something, and the cycle would start all over again.

There were also the financial issues. He bankrupted us once, and almost twice. He would steal money from our trust account. He maxed out all his credit, and then mine. I was so depressed and exhausted that I stopped looking or caring. I figured if I put one foot in front of the other, and all the children were alive at the end of the day, that was as good as it got. I became seriously depressed, and unable to cope. To the outside world, however, I looked perfect. I was very thin, and beautiful. I was outwardly vocal and confident. He threatened me that if I ever told anyone what was going on in our marriage, and what he was doing to me, he would hurt me. I wasn't allowed close women friends. He monitored all my telephone calls.

I finally connected with a good therapist. It took me two years to tell him what was going on in my marriage, for fear that my husband would find out I had "told." My husband would drive me to my therapy sessions, and pick me up afterward. He would debrief me on what I had talked about with my therapist. I am a lousy liar. On the day I told my therapist what was going on, my husband could tell that I had let the cat out of the bag. He berated and abused me. He threatened me. He told me he would ruin my legal career—and he very nearly did all of these things.

There was always the "pity play," as you say in your book—it was always my fault. I was so beautiful, I was so talented, that I made him feel inconsequential. He needed to feel more like a man. According to him, he had been abused by his father, his mother was crazy, I needed to make up for all of this stuff, and he was to be pitied.

I had a dream once about him early in our marriage. I

dreamed I was in a forest, and he was an animal in the forest. He was pitiable, pathetic. He was begging me to stay with him, or to take him home with me. When I hesitated, he turned on me. In my dream, he had teeth, and was ferocious. It was terrifying. I wish I had listened to that dream, and left him sooner. Instead, I stayed, and had four children, and suffered.

After he left, the enormity of the financial repercussions became apparent. He had stolen thousands of dollars from our trust account, which I had to put back. He had not paid any of the employee deductions to the government. He had not paid the Goods and Services Tax. We (meaning "I," since he simply walked away and refused to pay any of it) ended up owing thousands of dollars—about a hundred thousand, and that was before the mortgage. I paid it all off, every cent. I had to buy clothes for me and the children secondhand, even though I was earning a six-figure income. We lived in a very poor part of town until this year, and I have been separated from him for ten years. I have only just begun to have retirement savings, and I am now 52 years old, but I do not owe money like that anymore.

When he left, he dropped me like a hot potato. He took up with a client of mine, who was young enough to be my daughter. He forgot all about our four children for about a year, until he realized that pestering me about them was great sport, and a terrific way to upset me. He actually sued me for custody in the court and jurisdiction where I practice, knowing the humiliation it would cause. After I had to spill all of my sordid laundry to the judges that I appear in front of all the time—the whole record of all those times he abused and assaulted me—

*and once he realized he would lose, he dropped the lawsuit—
completely dropped it.*

*He married his new partner, and has started a replacement
family. He has four children (again). He has continued to harass
me regarding the children, but with the help of my therapist, I
have learned not to react. He has played games, like giving them
huge gifts, and allowing them freedoms that are not appropriate.
I have simply let that go. I can't fight that. He wants contact
with me, and the less contact I have, the better.*

*Through all the legal struggles, I have just held fast to my
parenting values, and trusted that my children would get it
eventually. I have not involved them, or engaged through them.
They all do get it, and I have had the privilege of parenting
them all. He really tried to get at me through them. I simply
refused to engage, and that seems to have worked.*

*I am happily remarried now to a lovely man who shares my
values. He loves my children, and they love him. I am largely at
peace. One of my old professors has been a mentor and friend
throughout all of this, and he supported me professionally even
when I was really weak, and doing poorly academically and
professionally. With his support and faith, I have managed to
achieve real success in my career.*

What did this woman do to come out of this ordeal with her
life on the mend and her spirit undefeated? The foundation of
her success was a self-educated understanding of what she was up
against: someone with no conscience. She learned what this person's (rather simple) motivation was: a craving to win at the
legal-system "game." She knew that his primary goal was to make

her jump, because her panicked reactions gave him a rush and made him feel like the winner. She was able to hold in her mind that his pattern—using and manipulating people and trying to make them feel sorry for him—had been the same since before she met him, and would remain the same always. And she appreciated the irony that his motivation in this "game" made him both irrational and predictable.

She did not try to prove his diagnosis to the court, and, after she got over her shock that psychological abuse was not considered by the state to be pertinent, she even stopped trying to prove that he psychologically abused his children. Instead, she did something more effective: she courageously endured the embarrassment of providing the court—her own workplace, in this case—with as much concrete information as possible about his abusive and violent behaviors toward *her*. Since she was reasonably certain she could predict his course, she gritted her teeth and stopped reacting every time he tried to use the children to make her jump. She dealt with him in the same way a parent must cope with a callous-unemotional child: by using contingency management. (In other words, *she stopped rewarding his appalling behavior with her overt panic*—and, as a bonus, stopped appearing to the court to be the "unfriendly" parent.) She asked for help, and learned to trust the people who valued her and treated her well. And in the end she got her self back; she was truly free, possibly for the first time in her life.

As this story illustrates, a person of conscience can be appalled by a legal game and yet, when necessary, be able to play it herself, rationally and with success. By any realistic appraisal, opposing a sociopath in court is a waking nightmare, particularly when children are in peril. But with persistence and an educated approach, you can live through the nightmare, and it will eventually end. Also, no matter what happens in the short term, remember that your children will greatly benefit from simply viewing the strength of your commitment to them.

WHAT NOW? A GUIDE FOR PARENTS FIGHTING A SOCIOPATH FOR CUSTODY

Here are my suggestions for the difficult and nearly surrealistic situation of dealing with a sociopath in a custody battle:

- Success requires giving oneself an education both in the game-playing patterns of sociopathy and in the location of hidden minefields in the legal system that may damage your case, such as the friendly parent doctrine and the vulnerability of the court to sociopathic lies (delivered coolly under oath).
- Be ready to educate your attorney as well, concerning the large body of research showing that physical abuse of one parent by the other does lasting harm to children who merely live in the same household.
- Keep a record of the insinuations, threats, and overt abuse that you yourself have suffered and can attest to without using psychological abstractions, and curb your natural wish to establish a diagnosis for him or her. Remembering that our legal system is concrete and non-psychological, you must restrain even your reasonable inclination to insist

to the court that he or she is "psychologically abusive" to the children.

- More demanding still, success takes courage, a practiced calm during an intensely emotional chapter of your life, and, in most cases, a willingness to live with uncertainty for long periods of time. I can assure you that an ability to be patient and to *wait* is an invaluable advantage over a sociopath, who by his nature is easily bored, drawn to immediate gratifications, and very unlikely to consider long-term outcomes. This is true even of sociopaths who are formidably wealthy.

- Most important of all—remember this about the sociopath's pattern: he has spent his entire life trying, in a wide variety of ways, to make people jump. Seeing others react emotionally to his machinations is immediately and intensely rewarding for him—strong encouragement to repeat his actions again and again. *Do not jump for him,* or at least do not let him see you jump, for the same reason that you would not leave out milk and cookies and a PLEASE COME AGAIN sign for a common house thief.

FIVE

THE ICIEST OF ALL

Assaultive and Homicidal Sociopaths

"I didn't know what made things tick. I didn't know what made people want to be friends. I didn't know what made people attractive to one another. I didn't know what underlay social interaction."

—TED BUNDY

Our attachments to other people structure our lives and arguably make them worth living: love for a new baby and a child's love for her parents; our place among the traditions, gossip, and loving hold of family and friends; the adolescent's preoccupation with "fitting in"; and later, the emotional tsunami of falling in love and the dream of a lifelong partnership of mutual love and support. Our brains are built for these attachments, from our soft spot for our pets to our strong connection with our human community.

As we have now seen, a mind that cannot form loving attachments develops a central preoccupation with having predatory power, with inciting (and witnessing) anger, fear, and despair. Inside a human mind that cannot love, there is only a compulsion to compete. Just as your life is organized around the desire to be close to other people, a sociopathic life is organized around a need to control, frighten, and elicit obedience. To accomplish this is to "win," and, for the loveless mind, winning is all there is.

Sociopaths who turn to lethal violence are in the minority. Most conscienceless people are destructive liars and manipulators who play brutal psychological, financial, and political games with our lives, and they comprise the single largest group of domestic abusers—which is to say, people who attempt to enhance their sense of power and control by beating up on spouses, children, and the elderly—but they are not often murderers. However, when they are, the results are severely disturbing.

BIND, TORTURE, KILL

The fact that a monster can look normal terrifies us. For this reason, an ordinary-looking man named Dennis Rader, a city employee, husband, and father of two, had an especially haunting effect on the public when he was discovered to be the infamous "BTK Strangler" (for "bind, torture, and kill") in 2005. Rader was finally arrested after committing ten grisly murders in and around Wichita, Kansas.

Rader was nearly everyone's worst nightmare. He was the workaday schlub, the churchgoing, Cub Scout–leading individual who, in his spare time, severed phone lines and tortured and murdered people. In the invisibility of his ordinary existence, he went undetected for thirty-one fear-clouded years. For all those thirty-one years, he lived in a neighborhood with his wife and children and went to work and to church with all kinds of everyday people. When at last he was caught and safely imprisoned, nearly everyone who knew him commented, "I just can't believe it."

We want our monsters to look like monsters. That we should want this makes good sense: if everyone who did hideous things looked like a person who did hideous things, we would know for sure that we were safe when we encountered people who looked like regular folks. But there is no face of evil. Pamela Smart, who conspired with friends to kill her husband, had been a cheerleader in high school. Notorious serial killer Ted Bundy was so handsome and charismatic that women sent marriage proposals to him on death row. The Parkland, Florida, school shooter, Nikolas Cruz, while in prison, has received romantic, sympathetic notes from girls.

We tend to conjure entirely the wrong images when we try to keep ourselves safe from those who commit horrors. Assaultive and violent sociopaths, though a small minority, constitute a compelling reason to raise our awareness of the sociopathic pattern.

Nationwide sentiment seemed to be that the suspect in the BTK murders had lived an ordinary life. But was that true? In retrospect, we can see that it simply was not. Dennis Rader had displayed symptoms of sociopathy long before he was apprehended. Of course, his monstrous deceptions were invisible until he was caught, but some of the other hallmarks of sociopathy had been conspicuous in his behavior all along. In fact, more eerily than anyone else I can think of, he was the sociopath next door. Modest in intellect and social position, Mr. Rader could not enter arenas such as high finance or international politics to play out the sociopath's will to dominate and win. Instead, he became the local dog catcher and the community "compliance officer." With his grant of a little power, photographs of their homes, tabbed and cross-referenced notebooks, and ruthless persistence, he aimed to control his neighbors' habits, their lawns and pets, their beers after work, and their language. He would give a sixty-nine-year-old woman a ticket for her loose dog, as she put it, "just because he could." When he confessed to the murders, he commented to the police that as a child he had often tortured animals.

We know that most people with a conscience do not spend their lives trying to make other people jump and comply. How many times have you picked up a yardstick and patrolled the lawn of your sick neighbor to judge the height of her grass? How often have you sneaked over to someone else's property and released the dogs, so that the owner could be cited? How many times have you sat with your friends at a bar and glared at them whenever they swore? Dennis Rader lived his whole life in such pursuits. And, in his humble way, he kept people's annoyance to a dull roar with his banal version of the sociopath's studied charm. According to a neighbor, on social occasions he "looked people right in the eye and said all the right things: that the party was lovely, the food was nicely arranged."

Conscience is a powerful emotion, a kind of evolutionary miracle. It is a sense of obligation based in our attachments to other people, and it keeps our behavior in line because we *feel bad* when we hurt someone. It is not an obsession with the rules—in fact, it sometimes causes us to defy the rules—and it is certainly not a conviction that one's own rules and ideologies are the universally correct ones. Most of us would feel guilty if we ate the last slice of pie in the kitchen, let alone if we deliberately set out to rob or harm someone, or to have her fined for a small infraction of the rules because it was entertaining—or, as Dennis Rader did, to strangle a stranger, let her breathe and feel hope for a moment, then strangle her some more until she could no longer struggle.

The absence of conscience—whether it be called sociopathy or psychopathy—is the psychological disconnection from the common well of human caring. Such detachment leaves only the desire to diminish and dominate one's fellows, the ultimate expression of which is killing them. The person who remorselessly torments his incapacitated neighbor over the length of her grass is not surprisingly the one who, with a little bloodlust added and his victims' lines of communication severed, can heartlessly kill. It is a story as recent as the headlines and as old as human history, a grim punch line that can be as local and everyday as our neighborhood and as large and seemingly unassailable as the heights of political power. So when we see someone who is driven to control and manipulate other people to the exclusion of any genuine compassion, and in the end we learn that the reach of his agenda included murdering them, perhaps we should not be quite so amazed.

The violent acts of sociopaths are not crimes of passion. To the contrary, sociopathic violence, like Dennis Rader's carefully thought-out murders—and like sociopathic behavior in general—is calculated, controlling, and cold. The following account, though it has a positive ending, is graphic and disturbing, and some may prefer to skip it:

> Richard and I met when were both seniors in high school. He was new, his family had just moved there. He had gone to five different schools growing up. The story he told me was that his father worked for a big company and got transferred to different cities all the time. Later I found out the real story.
>
> He was what we used to call a dreamboat back in the 1950s, so damn good-looking. I was kind of naive then. I was an only child and my parents had modest means. Richard lived in the wealthy part of town and had lots of money to throw around. He would take me out to expensive restaurants and buy me clothes from trendy shops. In a way, my loss of virginity was "bought" by him, I guess, after a piece of really expensive jewelry. I got pregnant 4 months later. I thought he might leave me then, but he was actually excited about having a child. My parents weren't happy about our shotgun wedding, but I was deliriously happy at the time.
>
> Things changed dramatically when we took up house together. I hardly ever saw him take a drink before, but now he drank heavily every night. I would gently chide him about it, but he just waved me off, accusing me of being "so naive." As time went on, he took less and less interest in our daughter and more interest in complaining to me. He would laugh at me when I tried to change her diaper, but never lifted a finger to help. Money wasn't a problem because his parents had set up a trust fund for him, but I kind of wish they hadn't. He didn't

even attempt to find work. He always acted like the world owed him something, like he was special, even though he wasn't doing anything much at all except making trouble for me. He would do things to humiliate me. Once when we were out at a bar, he pulled me into the men's room and tore off my blouse and bra, then left me there. I could hear him cackling with laughter as he left. I had to call a friend to rescue me. Later that night when I cried talking to him about it, he just waved me off, saying I couldn't take a joke.

Richard had seemed to purposely keep me away from his family, but I finally contacted his older sister and arranged to meet her for lunch. She told me that her family kept moving all the time because Richard had such a bad reputation. They were always looking for a fresh start that never came. I wondered what I had gotten myself into. But it seemed that just when I was ready to pack up things and leave with our child, he would revert back to the compelling man I first met.

Two years after the birth of our daughter, we had a son. Richard had been almost indifferent about our daughter, but now he became totally involved, in a bad way. He kept telling me how no son of his was going to grow up a sissy. He would wash him by taking him into the shower with him, ignoring his cries as the water pelted my poor boy. He would rattle the bars of the crib when he was in it. He wanted to toughen him up, he told me, pushing me away if I tried to stop him. The more I tried to keep Richard from acting this way, the more he would abuse me. I was forced to have sex with him almost every night. He even pulled the baby off my breast while I was feeding him once, so he could have his way with me that very moment.

At last Richard finally got a job, as a salesman at a local car dealership. That gave me the opportunity to pack up my stuff and take my children away. With help from my parents, I was able to rent a small apartment near them. He called me and threatened to take the kids away if I didn't come back at once. Before long he found out where I was. He came barging in because I had forgotten to lock the front door. He raped me on the kitchen floor and smashed dishes all around me while I cowered beneath him. He didn't even ask about the kids while he was there. Before leaving he screamed obscenities at me and told me he found a new woman who made me look like a hag.

One night I dropped my kids at my parents' and drove out of town. I was seriously contemplating driving off a nearby bridge into the river. But I drove back to my parents' and asked if we could stay there for a few weeks. I figured Richard wouldn't dare try anything there. And I felt so distraught that I didn't trust myself as a mother anymore. Thank God for my parents, who rallied for me then.

I began seeing a therapist and started feeling better. But my husband wasn't going to lay low through all this. He got a court order to take my kids. I couldn't believe this could happen, but he got them back. I knew that was just his way to hurt me, he could care less about our kids. I was so worried about how he might treat them. My therapist was great helping me get through this. I got a job and became a bit more stable. I was desperate to get my kids, but I had to wait for another hearing at the court.

I have to thank my daughter's behavior for getting her back. Richard got sick of her whining and brought her back to me. But he still had a hold on my son. About a month later he gave

*him back to me. He told me that I had infected him with
sissiness and that he was beyond repair. We divorced soon after
that, and I was convinced that I was rid of him for good.*

*Eventually I met another man, a decent man, and we got
married. Everything was fine for a year or two, but then out of
the blue Richard demanded visitation rights. The court allowed
it, unfortunately, and it was a traumatic experience for my kids.
They would always try to hide when he came over to pick them
up on weekends, and wept on their beds after he returned them.
When my daughter was thirteen, she refused to go. I found out
then that Richard had on numerous occasions forced her to strip
naked and dance around the room in front of his drunken pals.
He would throw baseballs at my son, very fast, from just a few
feet away to supposedly improve his reflexes. My son came home
with bruises from that and it turned him off from playing sports
of any kind.*

*Richard eventually remarried and my kids were able to shed
some of his influence. Both of them benefited from therapy and
were able to earn college degrees. They ended up getting married
and having children of their own. I thank God every day that
they were able to rise above all those years of horror at the hands
of someone they should have been able to trust.*

Reading this account, one wonders why, early on, the wife did
not simply leave. That she stayed as long as she did is a symptom
of *battered spouse syndrome,* a psychologically crippling reaction
to repeated trauma. The assaulted spouse becomes so shell-
shocked that she is terrified of leaving. An especially paralyzing
aspect of battered spouse syndrome is that the abused spouse

comes to believe she has brought her plight on herself—that she somehow deserves the abuser's brutal behavior—and that therefore she does not deserve to escape. The abuser caps all this off by assuring her that he is her only friend and protector, and that she would be completely alone and helpless without him. After each horror, he makes it clear that he will kill her if she tells anyone what is going on, and that no one will believe her anyway. Abetted by this insidious syndrome, violence can effectively hold people captive.

Because sociopathic violence is cold-blooded (done in a calculated way, without emotion), the sociopath is able to keep his aggression relatively concealed. Just as in the preceding account of a tortured wife and mother, the physical violence of the sociopath is often hidden—is domestic or "private" in some other way. Conspicuous acts such as those of the BTK Strangler notwithstanding, sociopathic violence tends to occur where we will not discover it. Horrific situations such as the one described above can play themselves out for years behind the closed doors of homes in unsuspecting neighborhoods.

Secrecy and eluding the law can be achieved in other ways as well. I have learned from the quantity of letters I receive on this subject that, as an especially alarming example, wielding an infectious disease as a weapon is often an invisible form of assault used by the cold-blooded. Far too many letters include revelations that someone knowingly had unsafe sex while infected with hepatitis or HIV. Factors that increase the risk of infecting others through sex include having multiple sexual partners and aggressive sexual techniques that tear mucous membranes and allow blood-to-blood contact. Perhaps the most disturbing aspect of sociopaths who assault in this way is that they *believe* they are transmitting a serious disease to other people and are gratified by that knowledge.

Any person searching for "love with commitment" is especially vulnerable to ruthless manipulators, and few are more vulnerable than someone who is struggling to align his relational life with his true identity:

> When I turned 30, I decided to finally accept who I was. I had always lived a heterosexual life, but it was unnatural for me. Finally, I summoned the courage to go to a gay bar. It wasn't long before I was engaged in hot discussion with Matt. I admitted to him that I had never had a sexual experience with a man. Matt seemed very compassionate. He told me he understood and that it was okay. It didn't hurt that he was very handsome and had a quick wit. He was hard to resist. We went back to his place and I had my initiation into a world that I had denied myself for too long.
>
> I was eager to see Matt again, and texted him the next day. Then the next day, and the next. I figured that I misunderstood his interest in me as a person. Then I went to the bar again and asked someone there if they'd seen him around lately. The bartender told me that he had been banned from the place. Matt had infected a number of men with HIV. He apparently knew he was infected but would tell his partners that he was disease-free so they wouldn't feel the need for protection. I talked to some other people in the bar and they confirmed that Matt

was a voracious sexual predator and had lied to a number of people about his health status. How could he knowingly do this to people, over and over?

Indeed, when sociopaths act out physically, their behavior often takes the same seemingly meaningless shape as that of non-physical sociopaths. Normal people do not see the point in it, cannot imagine why anyone would wish to do it, and frequently have a difficult time even believing it. Why gaslight an innocuous coworker? Why torture and murder a stranger? Why deliberately give someone AIDS? It is unfathomable to us. Sociopathic assaultiveness, like other sociopathic behavior, is all about winning for the sake of winning. "Winning" here is defined as manipulating and controlling other people. For the sociopath, power over others is mind candy, entertainment, and raison d'être all rolled into one. People with a conscience do not experience this motivation in the unalloyed way the sociopath does, and often will not recognize or acknowledge its manifestations.

IN COLD BLOOD

I want to emphasize the point that most sociopaths are not murderers. Most manipulate and control with lies and deception, mind games, legal games, threats, and interpersonal torment. However, when people without conscience do kill, they perpetrate the murders that shock us the most, for the very same reason that we have been discussing: sociopathy is ice-cold, emotionless. Sociopaths account for only 20 percent of our prison population, but that 20 percent includes the prisoners who have carried out the most depraved acts.

In 2002, the *Journal of Abnormal Psychology* published a report on data from 125 murderers, indicating that homicides committed by sociopathic offenders are "likely to be primarily instrumental (i.e., associated with premeditation, motivated by an external goal, and not preceded by a potent affective [emotional] reaction) or 'cold-blooded' in nature." The researchers found that, in contrast, homicides committed by non-sociopaths tend to be "crimes of passion" ("associated with a high level of impulsivity/reactivity and emotionality").

Sociopaths do not commit crimes of passion, as desperate and emotionally overwhelmed people sometimes do. They do not hear voices commanding them to kill, like the rare and tragic individual whose violent acts are compelled by paranoid psychosis. Rather, they murder for convenience and also because, for them, killing is exciting and fun—killing as the ultimate form of domination and control over another living being.

A sociopath with bloodlust is the closest thing there is to a genuine human monster. He can coldly plot the most satisfying way to murder and then methodically carry out the plan, whether it be against a complete stranger, a friend, a family member, or even his own child. Afterward, he can rationally calculate the best way to evade discovery. If he is caught, he can sit through a trial where his stomach-turning acts are described in front of other people, over and over and in gruesome detail, and display less of a reaction than someone else might show to seeing a rainy weather report on TV.

Ironically, it is just this icy rationality that sometimes convicts him. A review of forty-five years of research on how juries make decisions concluded that the best predictor of penalty outcome is the defendant's attitude during the trial process. If the defendant is seen as uncaring or nonchalant, disdainful or contemptuous, he is more likely to receive the death penalty. And jurors look at facial expressions and body language. The same study found that nonverbal displays of remorse, which suggest that the defendant is taking responsibility for his actions, are seen by jurors as more credible than direct verbal statements of remorse, which jurors seem to believe are more easily contrived.

This factor in jury decision-making is sometimes referred to as the "Scott Peterson effect," a reference to convicted murderer Scott Peterson and the jury that found him guilty in 2005. Peterson, a fertilizer salesman living in Modesto, California, was convicted of killing his wife, Laci Peterson, who was eight months pregnant with their child, tying her body to four ten-pound weights made of concrete, and throwing her into the San Francisco Bay. Four months after her disappearance, a couple walking their dog in Point Isabel State Park found a male fetus that had washed ashore. The next day, the body of a woman was discovered nearby, by another dog-walker. There was still duct tape on Laci Peterson's thighs. Her ribs had been fractured, and her hands, feet, and head were missing. As the mother's body had decomposed, her abdomen and uterus had torn, and the fetus's body had become separated from her own.

Evidently, Scott Peterson was preparing to flee to Mexico; the police arrested him in San Diego, and in his car they found $15,000 in cash, his brother's ID card, survival gear, four cellphones, and twelve Viagra tablets. Peterson was brought to trial and eventually convicted of the first-degree (premeditated) murder of his wife and the second-degree (intentional) murder of his unborn son. He was condemned to death and sent to San Quentin State Prison, where, as of this writing, he remains on death row, awaiting an appeal of his case to the California Supreme Court. He insists that he is innocent.

At his trial, through all the discussions of what had happened to the victims, and as he, the attorneys, and the jury were presented with the horrific photographs of the remains of his wife and his unborn child, Peterson remained detached, unmoved, even bored. In telling contrast, John Guinasso, Juror No. 8, would say later, "Viewing the autopsy photos in the courtroom was [an event of] mind-shattering disgust. Laci, this beautiful woman, was reduced to a piece of floating debris that washes ashore in the East Bay. It was very difficult to look at. These pictures would scar my mind for eternity." After the trial, some of the jurors suffered from post-traumatic stress syndrome. Some had flashbacks; others had nightmares. And yet, Scott Peterson himself looked unmoved during the six-month trial, and his unflinching iciness did not escape the jurors' attention. At some point, shouldn't this husband and father have shown remorse—or if he was innocent, some grief, or at least a trace of sadness?

The Scott Peterson trial renewed a long-standing debate in the legal community as to whether or not a defendant's courtroom behavior should be taken into consideration as valid circumstantial evidence. Some legal experts argue that a defendant's demeanor during the trial speaks to whether he is capable of the crime he is accused of and is therefore a valid component of the evidence, and others insist that courtroom behavior can be affected by extraneous factors and should not be considered. One can argue both sides of this legal question. But as a psychologist, I might point out that, as a matter of practice, juries and judges have been influenced by stone-cold reactions since King Solomon took up his sword and offered to slash a contested baby in half. The true mother shrieked "No!" in horror, and the fake mother thought he had a good plan.

As in the case of the BTK Strangler, the behavior of violent sociopaths observed *prior* to the discovery of their most heinous crimes is often the subject of debate as well. I frequently hear from readers who have been told that a victimizer is displaying "odd" behavior, or "textbook" behavior, or "red-flag" conduct, or activities that are "of concern," or that their tormenter is behaving in ways that are "possibly the onset of something"—but that nothing can be done because "nothing illegal has happened yet." Readers often report that they have uncovered instances of intimidation and violence in a victimizer's past—sometimes acts for which he was arrested and brought to trial—but are counseled that this is not "real evidence" in the present, and that they must "wait until a new crime occurs" for their concerns to be taken seriously.

Such situations constitute gaslighting by legal and mental health authorities, which, though inadvertent, compounds the deliberate gaslighting the victim may have suffered already at the hands of a cold and calculating individual whose potential for violence should be taken very seriously.

In recent years, as increasing numbers of school and university shootings have horrified the public, the issue of warning signs has gained some attention. Among too many examples, in

2008, a former sociology graduate student named Steven Kazmierczak stepped from behind a curtain onto the stage of a lecture hall at Northern Illinois University, faced a roomful of students listening to a talk on oceanography, and opened fire with a sawed-off 12-gauge shotgun and a 9mm handgun, killing five people and wounding seventeen more. Kazmierczak, called "Strange Steve" by the students in his former dorm, had studied the Virginia Tech and Columbine massacres and idolized "Jigsaw," the sadistic killer in the *Saw* horror films. On his right forearm, he wore a tattoo that depicted Jigsaw riding a bicycle through a pool of blood.

University of San Francisco professor David Vann, who researched the shooter's life, found that Kazmierczak had meticulously planned the shootings, and that throughout his life his behavior had included red flags that indicated he was capable of calculated violence. In the eighth grade, he made a bomb out of Drano and left it to explode at a stranger's house, for fun. Because he was "unruly" at home, his parents sent him to Thresholds, a psychiatric center in Chicago that specializes in psychosocial rehabilitation. He was thrown out of the Thresholds program for noncompliance and deception. He enlisted in the army, but was discharged within five months, for having denied on his application that he had a "mental illness." After that, he enrolled at Northern Illinois University, where his former roommates remember him as being obsessed with infamous murderers such as Adolf Hitler and Ted Bundy. In his book on Kazmierczak, Vann notes that, as the time of the shootings neared, the emails to acquaintances of the young killer-to-be turned to the subjects of mass murder and world domination.

Discussing Kazmierczak in a 2009 news interview conducted on the first anniversary of the NIU shootings, Vann remarked, "The degree of self-destruction and antisocial behavior at the end, of really scary behaviors, was just phenomenal. And at some point after you look at all of those records, you just have to wonder, what does a mass murderer have to do to get noticed?"

Cold-blooded violence and murder are not only the most complete form of domination; they are also the ultimate sociopathic manipulation of society. They make us all jump. In the aftermath of a mass killing, the worst possible reaction is the one we usually display: we broadcast, in all available media, the name of the killer, along with everything else about him that our able journalists can succeed in discovering. Out of our collective fear and prurient interest, the sociopathic murderer is fed a feast of attention like none other, along with detailed and even cinematic depictions of his astonishing power over ordinary human beings. From the homicidal sociopath's point of view, this is a last meal very much worth risking the death penalty for, and a win to be hungrily envied—and perhaps emulated—by others whose names are not yet known.

Like individuals who find themselves in child custody and workplace nightmares, we as a society must stop aiding sociopaths in extracting from us tremendous emotion for their entertainment and gratification. Media professionals and society in general must determine how we can handle information about sociopathic violence in ways that allow us to focus attention on the problem and its victims rather than on conscienceless perpetrators who try to "win" in this horrific way. One plan that has been suggested for the media is simply to speak the perpetrator's name as infrequently as possible in broadcasts, and to provide details about a killer only when such information is crucial and absolutely relevant to the event—no fame-making nicknames or acronyms: no Black Widow, no Jack the Ripper, no BTK Strangler. In contrast, information about the victims, including names and pictures, should be respectfully provided.

But there is a way in which sociopaths can now destroy lives without coming anywhere near their victims.

CYBERASSAULT

For the first time in human history, we can torment and victimize someone without direct contact. Cyberassault is not thought of as murder—although it has certainly led to suicides. It is a modern version of consciencelessness that relieves the assaulter of bloody hands. Done from a distance, sometimes anonymously, it gives the sociopath the same glee, the same happiness that he's ruining someone's life, as direct assault and victimization.

Computer science and other technologies advance so quickly that often we are not able to keep up with them emotionally, morally, or even legally. Our furiously changing circumstances have conferred myriad blessings of creativity and communication—and, frighteningly, they have accidentally provided new and almost completely unregulated playing fields for the conscienceless. Certain activities on these playing fields demonstrate that destroying a life can be done without even touching the victim and without any of the traditional weapons: no guns, no knives—just soul-crushing words and images on electronic screens. Among the most heartbreaking illustrations of the sociopath's coldness of heart are accounts of cyberbullying by adolescents and young adults. In cyberspace, efforts at deceit and predation are limited only by the imagination of the perpetrator. Here is one example:

> *Your book resonated with me strongly, because my child was victimized by a sociopath at his school. It began soon after we moved into the neighborhood. A kid two years older than him who lived next door launched an all-out assault on my twelve-year-old son with his Twitter account almost every day. He would send messages like "You should stop eating your own poop, you disgusting pig" and "What's the point of you even being alive?" He had pretty sophisticated graphic skills and would depict my son in humiliating situations that seemed real. We saved some of these tweets and showed them to the authorities to make them aware, but no action was taken.*
>
> *I mentioned these incidents to some parents of other kids, and they had their own stories to tell about my son's tormenter. This boy had a long history of meanness. I later met his parents. They admitted their son had caused trouble. They had tried everything with him. Taken him to therapists, had teacher conferences. He always turned on his angel act. He made it look like everyone else was overreacting or being overprotective.*
>
> *After the boy started high school and my son was still in middle school, our family heaved a sigh of relief. But the bullying didn't stop. He continued to spread false rumors about our poor son online, each one more vicious than the last. We told his parents, but they didn't know what to do about it. No one seemed willing or able to stop it.*

Our son became paranoid. He spent most of his time in his room, where he compulsively organized everything. He would gasp every time someone entered the room, always on guard for danger. Eventually we started looking into a different school. But it was too late. He killed himself on his 14th birthday.

Suicide is one of the largest causes of death in adolescents worldwide. Conducted in the Netherlands, a large meta-study (examining a number of preexisting studies to compare and analyze their findings) found an association between cyberbullying and suicidal ideation (thoughts of committing suicide) in 70,102 of 284,375 victimized adolescents. This project found also that this association was even stronger for cyberbullying than for traditional bullying, possibly because "wider audiences can be reached through the internet and material can be stored online, resulting in victims reliving denigrating experiences more often."

Unfortunately, the current status of anti-cyberbullying legislation—which involves even greater strategic complexities than workplace legislation—is not encouraging. In 2008, U.S. Congresswoman Linda Sánchez, a Democrat from California, introduced the Megan Meier Cyberbullying Prevention Act, named for thirteen-year-old Megan Taylor Meier of Missouri, whose 2006 suicide by hanging was attributed to repeated cyberbullying through the social networking website MySpace. The proposed legislation would make it a federal crime to send any kind of electronic communication with the intent to cause "substantial emotional distress." This bill died in committee.

Our legislators must do better.

To the suggestion that we need to teach children how to

handle being chronically tormented, Parry Aftab, a lawyer specializing in Internet security law and the executive director of Wired Safety, has said, "I don't want the kids to be more resilient. I want the kids who are doing it to stop. I want friends of the kids being bullied to stand up and say, 'I am with you.' The popular kids, the smart kids, the big kids need to stand up and say, 'Stop.'"

If you would like to help, or if you or someone you know is being bullied online, Aftab's website WiredSafety.com is a useful source of information and contacts.

WHAT NOW? A GUIDE FOR PROTECTING YOURSELF AGAINST A CYBERBULLY

- Understand that absolutely no one deserves to be bullied or abused. In other words, this is not your fault. This situation is the result of a disturbance within the bully, and not the result of who you are or anything you have done. He or she is just a garden-variety abuser, quite possibly a conscience-less one, who happens to be acting out online.
- Don't keep it to yourself; talk with someone about it—a good friend, a family member, a therapist.
- Change the privacy settings on your social media accounts; keep the things you share among friends only.
- Cut off every single contact you've had with the bully. Block the abuser's telephone number, his or her profile on social media, and his or her email address.

- Save proof of online bullying. Use the "print screen" or "screenshot" option on your computer to save evidence of cyberbullying, and install apps on your smartphone that will allow you to perform the same action there. You should also save copies of all emails that have been sent to you by the online abuser, from the very beginning until the present. You can show all this evidence to the police, should they become involved.

- Other than collecting evidence, ignore the bully if possible. Do not try to get even. The most aggravating thing you can do, from the bully's point of view, is to keep your cool. He or she will stop when bored with you and your apparent serenity. Pretend if necessary. Most particularly, do not return fire. You will succeed only in making the bully overjoyed that you are bothered and are reacting to the harassment. Keep the bully as far out from under your skin as you can.

- However, if you feel physically threatened in any way, even if it's just the whisper of a suspicion, gather your evidence and go to the police. They will know how best to proceed. Each state is a little different in its laws.

- Being abused in this way can sometimes cause people to feel so bad they actually want to die. If you begin to feel suicidal, or like harming yourself in some other way, tell your family and friends immediately. Let them help you. They love you. Do not allow this bully to "win."

I chose to devote these chapters to four types of situations with sociopaths—conduct disorder in children, sociopathy at work and in dealing with professionals, ex-spouses fighting for custody, and sociopaths who commit homicide and assault— because I receive stacks of letters and floods of email from people about these circumstances in particular. In the next chapter, I offer ten guidelines to arm yourself against these and all cases of sociopathy.

SIX

TRANSCENDING THE SOCIOPATH'S EFFECTS

Ten Key Guidelines

"We are at the very beginning of time for the human race. It is not unreasonable that we grapple with problems. But there are tens of thousands of years in the future. Our responsibility is to do what we can, learn what we can, improve the solutions, and pass them on."

—RICHARD FEYNMAN, "THE VALUE OF SCIENCE"

I n 1959, a Brown University psychologist named Russell Church published a scientific paper with the unlikely title "Emotional Reactions of Rats to the Pain of Others." This study found that rats trained to obtain food by pressing a lever would interrupt their lever-pressing when it was paired with the delivery of an electric shock to a rat in an adjoining cage. To some researchers, these small mammals appeared to be displaying what one might call *empathy* (the capacity to understand or feel what another being is feeling), an ability previously thought to be the property of humans only. Other psychologists hypothesized that the sight of another rat in pain simply evoked a fear reaction in the lever-pressing rat, causing it to "freeze." But, in 2006, a study at McGill University revealed that mice will show "empathic" reactions to the suffering of their cage mates only, and will not alter their behavior when exposed to the distress of mice who are strangers. This more discriminating behavior looks less like a simple fear reaction and somewhat more like our own tendency to respond automatically to family and friends, and much less automatically to people we do not know.

So, do rodents have empathy?

Yes and no, says animal behaviorist Frans de Waal. Rodents and the other "lower" animals are not capable of full-blown empathic responses, but they do possess the primal base for empathy—the relatively simple ability to apprehend another's emotional condition through the reflexive activation of their own neurological and bodily reactions. When an animal observes another animal's strong emotional state, its autonomic and motor reactions (respiration, heart rate, posture, movements, and so forth) mirror those of the emotional condition it is witnessing. This rudimentary sharing of another's emotions corresponds with the accumulating evidence for a link even at the cellular level between perception and action: the "mirror neurons," nerve cells that fire both when an animal acts and when the animal observes the same action performed by another.

De Waal proposes that empathy is comprised of three conceptual layers. The first and most universal of these is the physical, reflexive embodiment of the emotional state of another, as described above—a foundational component he calls *emotional contagion.* This first layer of empathy is responsible for the fact that both nonhumans and humans (sometimes even narcissists) appear to "catch" the emotions of others. Perhaps the most recognizable human example is that, when a baby begins to cry, other babies within earshot begin to cry, too. Most if not all social mammals, rats and mice among them, appear to be susceptible to this type of automatic emotional impact. The more similar and familiar the emoting individual is to his observers, the more likely it is that emotional contagion will occur.

The second layer of empathic ability, a component de Waal refers to as *cognitive empathy,* enables one to try to assess the situation and the reasons behind another's emotion. Cognitive empathy makes it possible to provide a response that aims to take the specific needs of the other into account. Chimpanzees and the other great apes and most humans have this higher cognitive ability. It is probable that certain large birds are capable of cognitive empathy as well. During his lifetime, Alex, the famously intelligent African grey parrot trained by animal psychologist Irene Pepperberg, provided us with many indications that this is the case. As but one poignant example, when a sad Dr. Pepperberg turned to leave her beloved Alex for treatment at a veterinarian's office, he is documented to have said, "Come here. I love you. I'm sorry."

The strong appearance was that cognitive empathy had led Alex to evaluate Dr. Pepperberg's behavior and to think she was leaving him because of something he had done to upset her. Based on his surmise, and hoping that Dr. Pepperberg might turn around, he said he was sorry (though apparently, like so many human apologizers, he was not entirely sure what he was being sorry for). Cognitive empathy allows us to know that someone is experiencing an emotion, but it does not provide specific information about what kind of emotion. Like Alex, we are left to make our best guesses.

The third and most advanced tier of empathy is the capacity to perform *mental state attribution*—the ability to adopt the perspective of another fully. Mental state attribution allows us to put ourselves in the shoes of another emotionally, and to provide what psychotherapists refer to as "accurate emotional empathy," a sometimes quite precise understanding of someone else's emotional state. Human beings vary considerably in their abilities at this highest form of empathic responsiveness. An individual who is especially gifted at mental state attribution can seem telepathic at times, but, rather than telepathy, a higher-order empath is accomplishing an emotionally acrobatic leap into another person's mind, not to "read" it, but *to understand how the other person is reading the world*. Accurately taking another person's perspective can inform an empathic person not just that the other person is experiencing an emotion, but also what the nature of that emotion is and why it is happening. Though an emotional empath is not clairvoyant, she or he can see the world clearly through the eyes of another.

Empathy, like conscience, is based in our ability to bond emotionally with others. An individual who is incapable of emotional attachment can possess neither conscience nor empathy. In sociopathy, the failure of empathy is complete; the dysfunction occurs at the most rudimentary level of empathy, that of emotional contagion. In their brains and bodies, sociopaths do not feel the reactions to the strong emotions of others that are experienced not only by their fellow human beings, but also by apes, grey parrots, and even rats and mice. In 2008, researchers at the National Institute of Mental Health conducted a meta-analysis of twenty studies concerning the sociopathic deficit in recognizing emotions as they are displayed in faces, and found that there is a reliable link between antisocial behavior and specific neurological deficits in recognizing fearful expressions, namely, dysfunction in the amygdala.

The emotion of gratitude as well is based in the ability to bond. In 1908, the sociologist Edvard Westermarck listed gratitude as one of the "retributive kindly emotions" that are the required building blocks of human morality. Gratitude is an enduring emotion, and usually a joyful one. Think for a moment about someone to whom, or *for* whom, you feel grateful: your child, or your own parent, a friend, a mentor, or even a stranger who made a difference, someone whose existence made a contribution to your day or perhaps your entire life. In your mind's eye, try to picture a face. How does thinking about this person—invoking this memory—make you feel?

Imagine having no sense of gratitude or thanksgiving, and understand that the truly ruthless are serving a life sentence in a joyless prison of ingratitude. Understand also that, for the same reason—the inability to form emotional connections with people—sociopaths have no emotional attachment to fairness and justice. Because a sociopath experiences other people as emotionally meaningless, he is completely unmoved when others are treated inequitably. Emotional investment in fairness and justice, gratitude, higher empathy, conscience—all of these emotional responses would appear to exist at the most advanced points in the evolution of the brain and mind. In bleak contrast, evil is a hole—a throwback—an empty space where the capacity to form interpersonal connections should reside, and this absence begets other fundamental absences. Evil reduces life, in all of its magnificent possibilities, to a mere game and a compulsion to win for the sake of winning. It mocks the human need for meaning that is found in such concepts as conscience, thanksgiving, justice, and love.

Conquering sociopathy—and elevating connection and love—is a grand human mission and a non-superstitious interpretation of the ancient struggle between evil and good, between love and emptiness. No matter who in your life you are fighting against—be it a coworker, your partner, or your own child—I want to give you the building blocks to mount a solid defense. As you consider the following guidelines for transcending the effects of sociopathy, view yourself as part of this human mission, as being on this positive vector, not just as a philosophical stance, but as a way to enhance your own personhood and well-being. And envision others doing the same, for I can assure you that there are others—hundreds of millions of others—who are on this path with you.

The best way to deal with a sociopath is to avoid him or her, to refuse any kind of contact or communication. The only completely effective way to protect yourself is to disallow him or her from your life altogether. Sociopaths live wholly outside of the social contract, and, violent or not, they are always destructive. But, unfortunately, it is not always possible to avoid the sociopath, even after he or she has been identified. Sometimes the sociopath is a parent or a sibling, or a ruthless ex-spouse from whom the children must be protected, or an employer or a co-worker in a job that is too valuable to leave. In some situations, simply getting away may be distressingly out of the question.

Here are ten guidelines for situations in which the sociopath in your life is impossible to avoid. These are the strategic principles that underlie the particular tactics described in the preceding four chapters. The first nine guidelines are intended primarily for taking on sociopaths who have not been physically aggressive, and who have not roused concerns about violence to come. The tenth guideline contains crucial instructions for dealing with sociopaths who have been violent with you or anyone else, made physical threats, or shown any other sign that they have a proclivity for physical aggression. You should take such signs very seriously. If you have reason to think that the conscienceless person you are dealing with may use violence, proceed directly to Guideline #10, and return to the previous nine principles after you have made yourself as safe as possible. *Making yourself physically safe is your first order of business.*

TEN KEY GUIDELINES WHEN YOU MUST FIGHT A SOCIOPATH

GUIDELINE #1: UNDERSTAND THE PERSON YOU ARE DEALING WITH.

Sociopathy is the complete absence of conscience. A sociopath can do anything at all without the slightest feeling of guilt, shame, remorse, or even embarrassment. He has no empathy, and will not react in any authentic way to your distress or anyone else's. In addition, he has no sense of gratitude, reciprocity, fairness, or justice. Overall, his psychological status is extremely difficult to comprehend; indeed, from the emotional perspective of a normal person, sociopathy seems impossible until you witness it firsthand. Therefore, *in order to deal with someone who is devoid of conscience, you will need to approach him using your intellect rather than your emotions.* Keeping your feelings at arm's length is made even more imperative by the fact that a sociopath may be exceptionally charming and flattering, or he may adopt a familiar demeanor meant to communicate that he is "just like you."

Never forget that, whether or not he is a physical threat to you, he is always psychologically dangerous. He will always lie in order to win, and if you have been targeted by him, "winning" means controlling you in some way—making you jump through hoops—no matter how vehemently he claims to have no such ambition. He will cause you to question your judgment, your perceptions, and perhaps your very sanity. You will need to remind yourself often of the objective information you have learned about sociopathy.

GUIDELINE #2: UNDERSTAND THAT YOU ARE ON THE SIDE OF GOOD; ENVISION A MISSION.

Examine your own personal ideas concerning the nature of evil, and then redefine evil in a more objective and less superstitious way for yourself. *Evil* results from the absence of an ability to form normal emotional connections with others. And, in counterpoint—according to all the major religions of the world and many other ancient sources of wisdom, and also by the implications of modern evolutionary thought—*goodness* exists where this ability to connect is present. In short, goodness stems from the power to love. If you have this capacity—if you are emotionally whole—then your conflict with a ruthless individual is part of a much larger contest, one as old as humankind itself.

Good, loving people are and always have been locked in a struggle against a deeply destructive biological, psychological, and spiritual glitch—an emptiness where human attachment should be. In your personal battle, you are on a mission that is older, larger, and more crucial than you may have imagined. While you are trying to cope, keep this concept of mission in the front of your mind. A focus on joining the larger mission of good people everywhere can sustain you in your individual struggle, even when giving in to despair offers its sweet but false promise of rest for the weary.

GUIDELINE #3: CHANGE THE GAME.

Any contest can be won or at least brought to a draw, even in the throes of defeat, if one contestant unilaterally and quietly changes the objective of the game. For instance, the usual goal in the ordinary game of checkers is to clear the board of all the opponent's game pieces; but what if one player secretly changes the goal? Let us say that there is a clever new player whose personal aim it is to take an even number of her opponent's pieces. With this unannounced new goal, she will probably succeed at her game well before her opponent can clear her off the board, no matter how skillful he is at the game he assumes he is playing, since all she will need to do is jump two of his checkers.

The sociopath's goal will always be to win, and he or she will invariably define winning as manipulating and controlling others. A complete lack of conscience makes him or her masterful at achieving this goal—much better at it than you can ever hope to be—and so you must secretly alter the premise. For example, if you are involved in a custody battle with a sociopath who is intent on maintaining control of you by using the children, do not try to "win." Instead, *try to keep the children safe*. Certainly, pursuing the goal of keeping them safe will involve trying to gain or keep custody of them, but this newly conceptualized purpose means that you will place only part of your energies into prevailing in court. (As we have seen, a courtroom seldom provides a level playing field anyway.)

Changing your perspective will allow you to direct more of your efforts toward remedies, however small, that are under your control: discussing problem-solving skills with the children if they are old enough, helping them to cope when they are not with you, enlisting the help of others who may be nearby when you are not, and—this is key—changing your own behavior so that you are less "fun to play with" for the sociopath. If you are less inclined to jump, less willing to spend all your time and every last penny fighting him in court, then he has lost some control over you already, and will tire of his game more rapidly. Similarly, if you are struggling with a sociopathic employer or coworker, do not try to "win" by gaining the upper hand or by exacting revenge. Instead, try to minimize the sociopath's daily effects on you.

In many situations, premise-changing can make all the difference for you, the people who care about you, and your sanity. Remember that you never wanted to play a domination game to begin with, and that, in general, winning for its own sake has never been the most meaningful aspect of your life. In contrast, your sociopathic opponent is utterly stuck in his conviction that winning by dominating is all-important. He is helpless to change his objective. If you are able to change yours, you will have a powerful advantage.

GUIDELINE #4: FOCUS CLEARLY ON YOUR OWN GOAL.

Focus on the goal you established for yourself according to the previous guideline. Compose a list of the objective or objectives that are more important to you than winning (keeping the children safe, keeping yourself safe, eliminating sociopathic stress at work, reestablishing peace in your life, and so forth). Write this list down, because you will need to see it again at times, to remind yourself of what you set out to do. Focusing on your list will work to protect you and those around you, and will lead you to a much more important and meaningful victory than simply beating up on the sociopath would have been.

GUIDELINE #5: DO NOT GIVE THE SOCIOPATH WHAT HE OR SHE WANTS.

The sociopath wants to manipulate and control you—to have a large effect on you—and so you are rewarding and encouraging him each and every time you allow him to see your anger, your confusion, or your hurt. While in his presence, strive to appear unaffected by the things he says and does. Practice a poker face and the art of speaking very calmly. You have a significant advantage in this strategy also, because the sociopath's brain processes emotional cues far less spontaneously than does the normal brain.

The sociopath wants a large, unmistakable reaction. Do not give it to him.

GUIDELINE #6: ENLIST OTHERS.

When good people get together and begin to feel comfortable sharing their ideas and experiences, the strange behaviors of a common acquaintance who is sociopathic will eventually become a topic of conversation. You may be surprised to find that you are not the only one who has been targeted. Not everyone will understand or accept an application of the term *sociopath*, but most people are at ease with expressions such as "manipulative," "too slick," and "liar." Do not insist on your own vocabulary or the terms used in this book. Speak more often of specific behaviors than of diagnoses. The words are not important. Allies are. There truly is strength in numbers, and the more allies you have, the better.

GUIDELINE #7: UNDERSTAND THAT THIS MISSION IS ONLY ONE PART OF YOUR LIFE RIGHT NOW.

The realization that one is being targeted by someone with no conscience often engenders a sense of panic, followed by an obsessive need to expose the deceit of the sociopath to others and put an end to his machinations immediately. Such a reaction, though understandable, can make dealing with the sociopath into a 24/7 concern, a preoccupation that can cause you to neglect the other, more meaningful activities and people in your life as you sink into the quicksand of your obsession. Pull yourself out of it. You may feel that you have dropped into the twilight zone, but you have not. This is just a sociopath, a cold and hollow individual who has decided to target you.

Though not an uncommon struggle, it may be a long one. You need to pace yourself. Your life—the sane and positive parts of your life—must go on. Do not allow yourself to devote your entire existence to a game designed by a sociopath.

I receive letters that tell of people losing their jobs, their friends, even their spouses—not due directly to the sociopath's schemes, but to the fact that the targeted person completely lost himself in the struggle and neglected everything and everyone else. Do not let this happen to you. Discipline yourself to think and talk about things other than the sociopath's latest incomprehensible actions. Do not alienate your friends and your family. To do so is to hand the ultimate "win" to the sociopath.

Be patient. Break your mission into doable tasks, and then make a contract with yourself *not* to do more than one of these tasks per day—or even per week. Examples of doable tasks might be:

Contact my boss and calmly tell her that I missed the meeting yesterday because John told me the meeting had been canceled.

Set up a file in my computer as a journal to record the alarming behaviors of my ex when he/she takes the children to his/her house.

Make a list of possible attorneys to handle the false accusation that has been made against me.

GUIDELINE #8: DO NOT CATASTROPHIZE.

Even in situations such as ugly custody battles, be realistic about the amount of damage that will or will not occur in the next day, the next month, the next year. It may be possible to do some significant damage control even before the battle is over (as in the "change the game" guideline), if you can remain pragmatic and reasonably calm. If you are constantly contemplating worst-case scenarios, anxiety and fear will freeze you in place.

There is an important corollary to this guideline: *Do not expect other people to rush or to work on this problem with the same passion you do.* Others are extremely unlikely to mirror your sense of urgency or your outrage, and if you try to convince them to do so, you risk losing their support altogether. Others will be more likely to help you if you do not present them with your panic and fear.

GUIDELINE #9: TAKE CARE OF YOUR HEALTH.

Being targeted by a predator, even or especially a human one, evokes the fight-or-flight response in animals and in people.

This essentially adaptive response is intended by nature to be short-lived—the animal either flees or makes a stand against the predator, both actions requiring all of the body's systems on alert to ensure survival. But when the predation is carried out over a long period of time, as is often the case in sociopathy, the physiological components of the fight-or-flight response become protracted: blood pressure and heart rate increase and remain high; stored reserves of fats and sugars are continually converted and released into the bloodstream (to supply extra energy to fight or run); muscles all over the body are tense; digestion slows and stomach acidity increases; slow and relaxed diaphragmatic breathing changes to fast and shallow chest breathing; and, beginning in the hypothalamus, a persistent chain of hormonal reactions stimulates the adrenal cortex to release unhealthily large quantities of stress hormones such as cortisol. For a while the body will attempt to adapt, but if it continues to be stressed, it will eventually succumb to exhaustion, immune system depletion, and illness. In other words, being targeted by a sociopath can make you very sick in the long run.

The best way to deal with this downward spiral (sometimes called *chronic stress syndrome*) is not to spin into it in the first place. If you have been targeted by a sociopath, consider a program of stress management to be a central part of your coping plan. The earlier you begin such a program, the better. Learn deep muscle relaxation, or practice meditation or yoga. Focus more on exercise or sports. Consider seeking supportive therapy. Do not let someone who is creating a major disruption in your life rob you of your physical and mental health as well.

I am often asked for referrals to therapists who specialize in treating the victims of sociopaths. Unfortunately, there is no such specialty at present. *Search instead for a therapist who specializes in treating psychological trauma survivors.* Such professionals sometimes identify themselves as providers of treatment for abuse and/or post-traumatic stress disorder (PTSD). While you are dealing with a sociopath and especially in the aftermath of your experiences with one, a skilled trauma therapist can offer support and a pathway to healing. Struggling with a sociopath often qualifies as psychological trauma, and you should seek a therapist who treats that problem. A trauma therapist's extensive understanding of sociopathy can be a nice bonus, but this specialized knowledge is unusual and not necessary for her or him to be of significant help.

GUIDELINE #10: PROTECT YOURSELF FROM VIOLENCE.

Typically, the sociopath will satisfy any appetite he may have for physical aggression by abusing family members in the privacy of his home, where there is little risk of discovery. In other situations, where there may be witnesses and/or obvious reasons to suspect him, external controls (the police and the threat of imprisonment) will usually compensate for his lack of internal controls (conscience and guilt). There are exceptions, however. If you have any concern at all about someone's tendency to use violence, take your sense of apprehension very seriously.

Do not keep your foreboding a secret. Whether your concern is for yourself or for others, a domestic issue or a public one, make sure that appropriate friends and family members are informed of your apprehension and whatever information you have. Referring to statistics on violence against women in his book *The Gift of Fear: And Other Survival Signals That Protect Us from Violence*, threat assessment specialist Gavin de Becker shares a frightening fact about the statistics on violence against women in particular: "Before our next breakfast, another twelve women will be killed. . . . In almost every case, the violence that preceded the final violence was a secret kept by several people."

If you have been overtly threatened, inform the police. Rather than merely calling or writing (which may not get the prioritized response you definitely need), walk into your local police station and, face to face, inform them of the specifics of the threat. You do not need to have proof. They may provide surveillance. At the very least, they will already have some warning and knowledge of your situation, should you need to call them in an emergency.

Make your home into a secure haven. Check to see that all doors and windows have strong, functioning locks, and use them at all times. Most important: If the sociopath comes to your door, *do not open it.* This can be a very difficult thing to do; our internalized prohibitions against being rude are surprisingly powerful. Be rude! Tell the individual to leave, and give him or her one chance to do so. If he or she does not leave with a single warning, call the police. (You may need to rehearse this action in your head prior to the moment of crisis, as summoning the police to deal with a "visitor" is something most of us are quite unused to doing.) In this situation, a sociopath may attempt to sway you with a pity play, such as "Please, I'm so upset. I just want to talk," or "Oh my God, please don't call the police! I'm so embarrassed." Do not be manipulated by the fraudulent emotion of a sociopath. Do not open the door. Do call the police.

Your concerns for other people are crucial as well. Always report child abuse and elder abuse to the appropriate authorities. Do this whether the abuse is occurring in your own family or you have reason to think it is occurring in someone else's family. There is nothing more important you can do for the larger human family.

The sociopath is winning each time you do any of the following:

- Fail to understand his true nature
- Play by his rules
- Lose sight of your real goals
- Let him see your anger, your confusion, or your hurt
- Remain isolated and attempt to go it alone
- Spend all your time and energy dealing with or thinking about him
- Lose your balance and set impossibly huge tasks for yourself
- Lose your patience (which is a virture you are developing)
- Allow yourself to panic or catastrophize (imagine outcomes far worse than any that are likely)
- Allow yourself to remain so stressed that your functioning is affected or you get sick altogether
- Lose your guiding sense of the meaning, history, and shared experience of what you are doing (your "mission")

Looked at the other way around, *you* are winning each time you do any of the following:

- Remind yourself of the objective information you have learned about sociopaths
- Reflect on the fact that your conflict with this ruthless individual is part of a much larger and older contest between human connection and hollowness
- Change the game on the sociopath (redefine what it means to win)
- Focus on your own goal instead of his
- Shield your emotions from the sociopath
- Strengthen ties with people who do possess conscience and empathy
- Divide your mission into doable steps
- Pace yourself
- Remain rational and pragmatic
- Attend to your health by practicing a stress-reduction technique

Remember that the sociopath suffers two major and interrelated disadvantages in this struggle he has initiated with you:

1. He is completely unable to conceive of "winning" as anything other than manipulation and control, and soon loses interest in any endeavor that does not involve winning in this way. You are more adaptable, in that you can decide for yourself what it means to win.
2. He has no automatic appreciation of the emotions of

others—no capacity for even the rudiments of empathy—but instead is limited to calculating others' emotions intellectually, the way a normal person might calculate answers to math problems. Therefore, with a bit of self-control, you can conceal from him what he is making you feel, thus hastening the advent of his most dreaded nemesis—boredom. Sociopaths report all the time to therapists, family, and others that they are frequently bored and crave extra stimulation almost continually. (Some use the word *addicted,* as in *addicted* to thrills, *addicted* to risk, *addicted* to making people react.) The sociopath's boredom is his looming lifelong adversary—and your best friend in dealing with him.

In the next chapter, I will cover one more topic people write to me about all the time: how to tell the difference between a narcissist and a sociopath.

SEVEN

SOCIOPATH OR NARCISSIST?

Recognizing Narcissistic Personality Disorder

> "But of course you must understand that rules of that sort, however excellent they may be for little boys—and servants—and women—and even people in general, can't possibly be expected to apply to profound students and great thinkers and sages."
>
> —C. S. LEWIS, *The Magician's Nephew*

Why is a keen ability to understand the emotions of other people considered a desirable psychological trait? Wouldn't it be wonderful to be immune to the ever-shifting feelings, the irrational highs, and the guilt-provoking lows of others? How much human energy would be conserved if we did not have to deal with the complicated moods of our friends, the emotional vicissitudes of our life partners, or the unpredictable psychological "phases" of our children? Often, there is seemingly nothing we can do to help others with their emotional lives, anyway.

Of course, it would not be desirable to have no conscience and no ability to love, for that would make you a cold-blooded sociopath. But what if we retained a conscience and kept the ability to feel the guiding emotion of guilt, along with our capacity to love and to bond, and were divested only of our ongoing sense of *other* people's feelings? How much do we really need to understand about other people's emotional lives in order to love and care for them?

Free of all that burdensome empathy, how would our lives be different? And what would a condition of emotional ignorance feel like? As you'll soon learn, it's not nearly as simple and peaceful as you might think.

To convey an understanding of complete emotional nonawareness—for such a condition does exist—I invite you to fantasize for a moment that you are inside the head of someone whose mind, though not sociopathic, is still radically different from your own. Imagine that you are totally unable to perceive the emotions, wishes, and motivations of other people, and that you have always been oblivious in this way. Indeed, rarely have you recognized that others even *have* feelings. Due to this condition of yours, facial expressions, body language, and tones of voice are at best foreign languages. These interpersonal signals, ones toward which most people exhibit an excruciating sensitivity, almost always fly past you unnoticed. Emotional signs that are simply too conspicuous to miss—for instance, the tears of other people—make you nervous and sometimes angry. They are utterly bewildering to you.

And because the emotional responses of others—responses that you cannot interpret at all—comprise much of what ordinary people use to make inferences about one another, you can form no completely reality-based appraisal of anyone. You are missing a large part of the information—the emotional part. This limit on reality-based perception allows you to know individuals only as what you believe them to be, which is to say that other people become, to a disabling extent, figments of your own mind. If *you* think he is brilliant and a leading authority on a subject, then he is. If *you* believe she is a goddess and the woman you were born to spend your life with, then, in your emotionally sealed-off world, she is, regardless of her true nature and her feelings on the matter. You are thoroughly seduced by your own ideas and wishes concerning other people, and impermeable to any real-world emotional reactions on their part that might challenge your foregone conclusions.

The only true feelings you can perceive are yours. Like most people, you are capable of desire and fear, seething hatred, compelling love, excruciating guilt. You know anger, jealousy, and full-blown lust—but only your own. When they are displayed by other people, you are as blind to these emotions as you would be to the pages of this book in a pitch-black room, and when others try repeatedly to explain their feelings, you are deaf. To top it off, you are blithely ignorant of your own limitations, unaware that anything is missing in the way you perceive and relate to your fellow human beings.

The irony of your life is that, even more intensely than emotionally healthy people, you desire to be near others and, especially, to be recognized and appreciated by them. You tend to become painfully depressed when left alone, sometimes turning melancholic within only a few hours. You want to be part of a couple, or if you are partnered already, you wish to remain that way till death do you part. If you have children, you want them to admire you. You imagine your coworkers and associates speaking of you as an exceptional person with whom they love to spend time, and you regard yourself as someone who pursues the goal of lasting friendship. But unbeknownst to you, you are not emotionally equipped for any of these interpersonal successes. When you have long-term relationships at all, it is only through the forbearance of other people, or their poverty of self-esteem, or their weary resignation to your cluelessness—or, if you are highly placed in the world, their interest in your power.

The many lost relationships in your life are an exasperating mystery to you. Try as you may, you have not been able to find any rational explanation for why so many people have left you over the years. Why do people start screaming at you, often claiming that you are a bad person, when you have done nothing at all to them? You pride yourself on being loyal and reasonable, so how do you keep winding up with others who are erratic and accusatory? In an incomprehensibly turned-around way, people in the process of shredding a bond with you call *you* destructive. Once, a former lover even screeched at you that you ruin other people's lives. If you could figure out what was causing others to turn on you like that, to say such crazy things, no doubt you would fix the problem. But when you ask them what's wrong, they give baffling, illogical answers. So far, the only explanation you can credit is plain bad luck. Perhaps you have just met all the wrong people. Or maybe people are just unable to appreciate how special you are.

This is the inner world of the *narcissist,* how he interprets his interpersonal failures and the often extensive damage he does to other people, especially those most valuable to him. Lacking access to a supremely important category of information—the emotions of other people—the narcissist is stuck in a kind of time loop: he creates the same interpersonal disasters over and over again, almost always losing his closest relationships, and is fated never even to glimpse the reason why. Underneath his seamlessly self-involved exterior, blind and deaf to what makes his fellow beings tick, he spends most of his life in an inner world of bewilderment, torment, and often rage.

Narcissistic personality disorder is a condition without the amoral overtones of sociopathy, but it's important to be aware of the differences and similarities between the two. The damage done by a narcissist may be equally appalling to a close friend, a business associate, or a life partner, all of whom may come to be just as desperate to get him out of their lives. The narcissist can love his children, but, sadly, he is also likely to deal them lifelong emotional wounds. Some of the behaviors and particular forms of destructiveness associated with the extreme narcissist can be virtually identical to those of the sociopath.

I have received many messages such as this one:

> *No one likes my boss much. I used to think he was a*
> *narcissist, but now I'm not sure. When anyone disagrees with*

him, he basically hates that person from then on and trashes them at every opportunity. He went so far as to get some of these people fired. He also talks about a lot of personal things in his life. I can't tell you how many times I've been held captive in his office while he went on and on in agonizing detail. He seems unable to recognize when someone's not interested. It seems like the better you do your job, the more likely you're in danger of him turning on you.

His infatuation with himself is bad enough, but his lack of empathy makes him downright cruel. When someone in the office had to take a leave of absence for chemotherapy, he actually scoffed, as if the whole thing was just a way to get out of work. When she returned with significant hair loss, he joked that the office was going to take up a collection to get her a toupee. I've given up trying to connect with this person, unless it's essential for work.

This supervisor's lies and his coldness toward those whose dismissals he causes, and toward a cancer patient, are behaviors that bring sociopathy to mind. But his habit of telling excruciatingly detailed stories about his life to people who are at best humoring him, could indicate narcissism. So which label, if either, is accurate?

The fundamental difference between sociopathy and narcissism is an important one, but can be surprisingly irrelevant in the real world: *Where the sociopath is devoid of both conscience and empathy, the narcissist lacks "only" empathy.* In other words, the sociopath can neither form feelings of connection with others nor directly perceive their emotions, whereas the narcissist cannot perceive the emotions of others but *can*, in his way, form interpersonal bonds. *Because he has the capacity to bond, the narcissist does experience the emotion of conscience. But his ability to act on that conscience is severely flawed by his impenetrable ignorance of other people's feelings and needs.*

All of us need a certain amount of normal self-regard ("healthy narcissism") to develop normally and thrive in adult life, but when that feeling grows out of proportion and overwhelms other feelings, we come to suffer from narcissism. When narcissism grows so large that it hurts relationships and other people, some professionals call it *pathological* or *pernicious* or *malignant* narcissism. When a person is referred to as simply *narcissistic,* the usual implication is that his relationships and the people in his life are being harmed and that the word *pathological* would apply.

IS IT NARCISSISM OR SOCIOPATHY?

The *Diagnostic and Statistical Manual of Mental Disorders IV* of the American Psychiatric Association (*DSM-IV*) defines narcissistic personality disorder (NPD) as a "pervasive pattern of grandiosity (in fantasy or behavior), need for admiration, and lack of empathy, beginning by early adulthood and present in a variety of contexts," and states that a diagnosis of NPD may be indicated if an individual exhibits five or more of the following nine symptoms:

1. Has a grandiose sense of self-importance (e.g., exaggerates achievements and talents, expects to be recognized as superior without commensurate achievements).
2. Is preoccupied with fantasies of unlimited success, power, brilliance, beauty, or ideal love.
3. Believes that he or she is "special" and unique and can only be understood by, or should associate with, other special or high-status people (or institutions).
4. Requires excessive admiration.
5. Has a sense of entitlement, i.e., unreasonable expectations of especially favorable treatment or automatic compliance with his or her expectations.
6. Is interpersonally exploitative, i.e., takes advantage of others to achieve his or her own ends.
7. Lacks empathy: is unwilling to recognize or identify with the feelings and needs of others.
8. Is often envious of others or believes that others are envious of him or her.
9. Shows arrogant, haughty behaviors or attitudes.

With the publication of the *DSM-5* in 2013, the approach to diagnosing narcissistic personality disorder changed. As a part of this new conceptualization, NPD is said to involve the following "impairments in interpersonal functioning":

- *Empathy:* "Impaired ability to recognize or identify with the feelings and needs of others; excessively attuned to reactions of others, but only if perceived as relevant to self; over- or underestimate of own effect on others"

- *Intimacy:* "Relationships largely superficial and exist to serve self-esteem regulation; mutuality constrained by little genuine interest in others' experiences and predominance of a need for personal gain"

In addition, according to the *DSM-5*, NPD is marked by the following "pathological personality traits":

- *Grandiosity:* "Feelings of entitlement, either overt or covert; self-centeredness; firmly holding to the belief that one is better than others; condescending toward others"
- *Attention-seeking:* "Excessive attempts to attract and be the focus of the attention of others; admiration-seeking"

The icy coldness of sociopathy results in large part from congenital deficits in the brain's ability to process emotional and interpersonal input. The lack of empathy in narcissism is thought to result primarily from a shortfall in the emotional connection between a small child and his or her primary caregiver, who also may be abusive and/or narcissistic. In this case, the normal development of the limbic-brain areas involved in empathy and compassion is disrupted by a dysfunctional caregiver's failure to reflect back to a young child the emotions he is experiencing (as in, "Seems like you're feeling mad"). The emotional dysregulation that results in pathological narcissism is thought to be induced between birth and the age of about two years, as opposed to the emotion-processing deficit in sociopathy, which is partly genetic. This means that the failure of empathy in narcissism versus that in sociopathy is analogous to, for example, having an arm seriously damaged in early childhood as opposed to having been born without an arm.

The failure of empathy in sociopathy is complete. Sociopaths do not experience even the primal reaction of *emotional contagion* (reflexively "catching" the strong emotions of others) that is displayed by other people and other social animals. Even a baby will cry if she hears another baby crying. The narcissist, in contrast, does sometimes experience emotional contagion, though he is less susceptible to its call than the rest of us are; his self-involvement tends to shield him from even this rudiment of empathy. Interestingly, however, some clinicians, myself among them, have observed that narcissists are better than most of us at generating emotional contagion in other people. Like water boiling in a tightly lidded pot, their grandiose emotions and beliefs about themselves—sealed off from input from the rest of the world—can become so intense, so expansive, that they can overflow and influence others.

In *The Destructive Narcissistic Pattern*, clinician Nina Brown notes that some people are more vulnerable than others to the emotional contagion created by narcissists: "Susceptible people tend to attend to others' emotions rather than ignore them, perceive themselves as interrelated with others rather than completely independent, are adept at reading nonverbal emotional behavior or communication such as voices and gestures, tend to assume the bodily expressions of others when talking with them, are emotionally self-aware, and are emotionally reactive." Differently stated, it is the extremely empathic who are most likely to "catch"—and perhaps be overwhelmed by—the emotions of the narcissist.

If you are exceptionally empathic, and especially if you feel that your life has been waylaid by one or more narcissists, take note. Protracted exposure to an extreme narcissist can "infect" empathic people with the narcissist's fantasies—grand visions of unlimited success, power, brilliance, beauty, or ideal love—and can draw usually sensible people into business, political, legal, and relationship disasters they would ordinarily steer clear of. The emotional radioactivity of narcissism often furnishes narcissistic political leaders, ideologues, and self-serving "great thinkers and sages" with passionate disciples and believers. Indeed, on a group level, one technical difference between a sociopathic leader and a dangerous narcissistic leader is that the sociopath influences through lies, manipulation, and threats, whereas the narcissist influences through lies, manipulation, and emotional contagion.

When people ask me about sociopathy, narcissism, and politicians, I respond that I don't support diagnosing anyone I have not spent face-to-face time evaluating. But I will say that if a patient came to me who exhibited the personality traits that we have seen in Donald J. Trump as president of the United States— the grandiosity, the utter absence of empathy, the excessive need for attention and admiration—I would think long and hard about narcissism.

The malignant narcissist is motivated primarily by the need to have others admire him, to collect recognition and accolades from the outside world, and to hear only positive regard and praise from the people around him. To keep his inner world intact, he needs others to accede to his belief that he is innately superior and therefore worthy of special dispensation, whatever his behavior may be. He is driven to find constant admiration and compliance, and evaluates other human beings in terms of their capacity and willingness to be such sources. The narcissist does this less consciously than the sociopath but experiences it more solidly than most people do. The sociopath's need is for power; the narcissist's is for praise.

The psychoanalyst Otto Fenichel stated, in 1938, that the narcissist "requires a 'narcissistic supply' from the environment in the same way as the infant requires an external supply of food." When another person, or the world at large, comes across with criticism or a reality concern, he experiences what psychoanalysts refer to as a "narcissistic injury"—a psychological threat to his fragile but all-important inner world. Typically, the narcissist will respond to such an affront, even a seemingly slight one, with a primal rage—a seemingly inexplicable white-hot fury that initially feels frightening to other people.

In the real world, as opposed to the clinical one, the major discernible difference between narcissism and sociopathy is the distinction between *hot and cold behaviors*. The sociopath exploits others using behaviors that are cold, emotionless, and calculating, including (in most circumstances) a studied charm. The narcissist exploits people, too, but through emotional behaviors that arise from an ironclad belief in his own superiority and a certainty that he deserves unlimited success, power, brilliance, beauty, or ideal love. When frustrated by criticism or the noncompliance of other people to his wishes, the narcissist becomes heated, rageful, hateful. The sociopath simply goes back to the drawing board, tweaks his plan, and pours on more charm or perhaps additional threats. The narcissist can be a passionate, compelling, and immensely destructive ideologue. The socio-path has no ideology at all; his destructive behavior is icily logical and aimed only at winning the "game" of domination. Seldom will he jeopardize his game by losing control of himself, and never by fiercely guarding an emotional castle in the sky.

If your life has been mauled by a sociopath, you have been intentionally and coolly targeted by a person who can do any-thing at all without the normal emotions of guilt or shame. If your life has been mauled by a narcissist, you are the casualty of a person who is warmer, but who inevitably turned (or will turn) your relationship into a well of narcissistic supply that he inevi-tably drains dry. This is someone who, in his endeavor to keep his false inner world intact, can do *anything* with little compre-hension of the pain and damage he is causing.

Both sociopaths and narcissists are exploitative, and the dif-ferences outlined here can seem subtle. Certainly, the damage can be just as extensive in either case. However, close up and personal, there do tend to be differences in how normal people react to these two personality types. With both sociopaths and narcissists, there is usually a honeymoon phase at the beginning of a relationship, in which the disordered person can seem "too good to be true" (and when people seem that way, they often are). In a relationship with a sociopath, the victim typically be-gins to feel that something is wrong that he cannot quite put into words; things are not quite adding up. The victim may start to ask questions, to which the sociopath responds with redoubled seductive charm, or threats, or both. The victim feels bad about himself, confused, and *anxious*. After the honeymoon phase with a narcissist, the victim begins to feel, and accurately so, that the relationship has become all give and no take. The victim typically initiates countless conversations intended to explain to the narcissist that he is not meeting the victim's emotional needs. These conversations are wasted breath. The victim feels bad about himself, confused, and *angry*.

Typically, a relationship with a sociopath ends with the discovery of some act of deceit that is too great to be ignored or reinterpreted. It is at this point that a victim may look into the sociopath's eyes and realize with a shock, as many patients tell me, that his eyes are "predatory" or "scary"—the eyes of a stranger, which makes him easier to leave. A relationship with a narcissist can be stickier; the victim may continue, sometimes for years or decades, to try to talk the narcissist out of his narcissistic behaviors, to shout and cry, to explain what the narcissist "must" do to correct the damage he is causing. The victim typically loses all respect for the narcissist, and comes to see him as ridiculous, weak—a permanent "child."

In the end, the victims of narcissists tend to feel a threat of contamination and general disgust (as did the narcissist's victim who told me she might need to purchase some "industrial-strength douche"), versus the victims of sociopaths, who typically perceive a threat of direct harm, physical or otherwise.

I receive letters asking me whether sociopaths might have "a little bit of conscience." Some of these letters all but plead with me to say that they can, to supply a grain of hope. Sadly, sociopaths cannot, by definition. These messages list instances in which a sociopath behaved in ways that seemed to be conscience-driven. I suspect that some of the individuals who ask me this question are dealing not with sociopaths, but with narcissists, who do indeed have "a little bit of conscience." Unfortunately, though this looks hopeful on paper, it may serve only to make a relationship with a narcissist even stickier than usual.

Reflecting back on time spent with a sociopath, people often employ words such as *chilling*, *predatory*, and *criminal*. When speaking in retrospect of the narcissist, they tend to use words such as *maddening*, *loser*, and *idiot*. (Interestingly, for both the sociopath and the pathological narcissist, people use words such as *devastating* and even *monster*.) Sooner or later, the sociopath elicits anxiety and fear. In contrast, beginning early on in any relationship, the narcissist seems clueless, which is truly maddening. Victims speak of screaming at him, or of wanting to take him by the shoulders and shake some sense into him. Even trained clinicians tend to get angry with narcissists, and must be on their guard in the session room.

Technically, all sociopaths are narcissistic. The antisocial personality disorder listing in the *DSM-5* includes "lack of concern for feelings, needs, or suffering of others" and "incapacity for mutually intimate relationships" as the disorder's impairments in interpersonal functioning. Upon close scrutiny, we can see that of the seven pathological personality traits of antisocial personality disorder reviewed in chapter 1—manipulativeness, deceitfulness, callousness, hostility, irresponsibility, impulsivity, and risk-taking—really only three (hostility, impulsivity, and risk-taking) cannot easily be accounted for by the sociopath's narcissism. This means that, when we are trying to sort out the sociopaths from the narcissists by this clinical method, we are looking primarily for *hostility* ("mean, nasty, or vengeful behavior"), *impulsivity* ("acting on the spur of the moment in response to immediate stimuli"), and *risk-taking* ("engagement in dangerous, risky, and potentially self-damaging activities, unnecessarily and without regard for consequences") as the extra characteristics that denote full sociopathy.

A narcissist is cruelly unresponsive to the emotional needs of his children, his friends, and his lovers, and often leaves long-term scars. In contrast, a sociopath—who also leaves long-term scars—studies people's emotions as you or I might study math or a foreign language; he knows exactly how to respond. In inter-personal situations, this skill can make a sociopath more difficult than a narcissist to distinguish from a normal person, because both the normal person and the sociopath seem to respond compassionately to the distress of a family member or a friend. In other words, in many situations where the narcissist would be clueless, unresponsive, and perhaps annoyed, *the sociopath will be responsive,* often charmingly so, creating a better disguise than the narcissist has. Typically, the only situations in which a socio-path will not be responsive are when he is trying to gaslight someone using silence and when he is finished "playing" with someone.

Imagine two lovers walking down a steep and icy street on a wintry day. He watches her to make sure she does not slip, and in doing so, he himself falls and breaks his arm. Tears of pain fill his eyes, and he asks her to get him to a hospital. She is a narcis-sist. Her arm is not broken, and so, in her cosmos, there is no pain—just inconvenience.

She says, "It doesn't really look that bad to me. Let's keep going. You'll probably start to feel better in a minute."

Only after ten minutes of arguing does she finally hail a cab and take him to an emergency room, complaining the whole way about the bother.

Now imagine a second couple on a similar icy street. He falls and breaks his arm and asks to be taken to a hospital. But this fellow's companion, beyond narcissistic, is a sociopath.

She says, "Oh my God, you poor thing! We need to get you to an emergency room *now*!"

Seemingly all compassion, she hails a cab and gently helps him into it. When they get to the hospital, she assists him through the check-in process and remains solicitous until he is finally called in to get an X-ray. A doctor gives him a painkiller in the examining room and sets his arm and he starts to feel a little better, but when he returns to the waiting room to rejoin her, she is gone. He manages to get himself home and does not see her again for four days. When she finally shows up, she is full of concern and apologies. She says that while she was in the waiting room she got a call from her sister, who was very ill. She rushed to another city to be with her and was so distraught that she forgot to call him.

In actuality, she spent those four days with another man, one who was not incapacitated by a broken arm. She had thought this new lover might be rich, and then discovered he was not.

Or consider a different situation:

This couple lives together, at her place. He is unemployed, having been fired because he alienated his boss, and she is supporting them both. He has cooked a romantic dinner for her, and proposes marriage. He tells her she is the only woman in the world who has ever understood him. But then she mentions that she has just purchased a new suit for work. He flies into a rage because she did not ask him first. He is so angry that she becomes frightened and ashamed, and promises that, when they are married, she will always ask his permission before any big expenditure.

His behavior strongly implies narcissism.

Now consider a second couple, also living together at her place. This fellow has been unemployed for years, because he is "too sensitive and creative to work at a regular job." She supports them both. He has cooked a romantic dinner for her, and proposes marriage. He tells her she is the most beautiful woman he has ever seen. She mentions that she has just spent some money on a new suit. He is extremely supportive of her purchase, and announces that "they" should splurge on a nice restaurant soon, so she can wear her new clothes.

They will have been married for two years before she figures out that he is a sociopath.

MORE SIMILARITIES AND DIFFERENCES

Being aware of some of the other similarities and differences between sociopathy and narcissism will give you a more complete understanding of both disorders.

Lying and deceitfulness comprise the centerpiece of both sociopathy and destructive narcissism. The sociopath lies to obfuscate, to manipulate others into bending to his will, and for fun. The narcissist lies to maintain his false world and to manipulate others into being sources of narcissistic supply (constant admiration and compliance). In common parlance, both are sometimes referred to as "pathological liars," and in both disorders, deceitfulness is the primary tool used to exploit others. The sociopath is a con artist, and the narcissist resides inside a false persona. Continual lying is required in both cases.

Both sociopaths and narcissists are intensely competitive. The sociopath lusts after control and power; he is single-mindedly focused on winning for the sake of winning. The narcissist is compelled to one-up everyone else in order to prove his superiority; he is pathologically jealous of others' strengths and accomplishments.

Both may behave in ways that bespeak grandiosity, abnormal self-assurance, and an inflated sense of self-importance.

Both are shame-proof and often even embarrassment-proof. In the case of the sociopath, this is because he literally does not experience shame or guilt, consciously or unconsciously, no matter what he does. The narcissist can experience shame, but will defend his psyche against it with every ounce of his being, because shame is the single most ominous threat to his false inner world. The narcissist's carefully cultivated sense of superiority and his refusal to admit any sense of shame into his consciousness are the roots of his trademark arrogance.

Both sociopaths and narcissists consider themselves to be above all laws, social conventions, and moral principles. The narcissist feels he is above the law due to his general sense of entitlement. The sociopath sees all laws and expectations as games to be played.

Upon meeting someone in whom they have an interest, both may push for "instant intimacy." The narcissist may be in a rush to subsume someone into his false world (wants to marry him or her after a first date, for example). The sociopath may wish to take advantage of someone's initial ignorance of his true nature. Both hate the signs of normal autonomy in a victim. Both may try to alienate the victim from his or her family, insist that he or she not see friends, and so forth.

Both of these pathological personalities commit interpersonal "crimes" by using the word *love* as a bargaining tool or a weapon.

Both tend to gaslight people who are close to them (make them feel they are losing their minds). The sociopath does this intentionally and maliciously. The narcissist gaslights less consciously, through his very way of being in the world. He experiences other people primarily as extensions of himself (as does the human infant). And his behaviors in a close relationship—his enacted belief that he suffers in this life more than other people do and that the victim is his indispensable protector and keeper, his projection onto the victim both of his grandiose fantasies and his self-loathing, and his idealization of the victim juxtaposed with continual harping and criticism—can induce the person in a relationship with him to lose his or her own psychological boundaries. Eventually, the narcissist's long-term victim may feel unable to leave or to set any other self-protective limits with his or her psychological captor.

Both sometimes attempt to manipulate a victim long after the victim has ended the relationship, for months or even years—the narcissist because he is driven to maintain his illusory inner world (in which the victim has no existence separate from his own), and the sociopath because he considers the victim to be his property. This after-the-fact behavior does not always occur in either case, but when it does, it can be as frustrating or frightening as the original exploitative behaviors were.

However, sociopaths possess none of the higher emotions. Narcissists do have these feelings, but their lack of empathy warps the expression of emotions in ways that make their presence useless at best, destructive at worst.

Sociopaths always do what is best for themselves without considering others, because they have no conscience. Narcissists always do what is best for them because, in their minds, what is best for them is best for the world.

Upon discovery, the sociopath will always deny responsibility because outright denial often works (especially if they've been gaslighting all along). The narcissist also usually denies responsibility, but this is because he cannot tolerate any explanation of events that is at odds with his mental construction of himself and the world. He reframes all situations to make them fit into his false vision, and if necessary will do so in elaborate, crazy-sounding ways. The narcissist confabulates; the sociopath simply denies, and is usually more clever and more charming ("slick") about it.

Occasionally, the narcissist will take responsibility when he believes he has failed within *his own worldview*, or behaved in a way that violates *his own construction* of good and bad. The sociopath loves to manipulate and simply does not care that he has hurt someone. The narcissist does not wish to hurt others, but is psychologically blind to their feelings (and often to reality), which means he may easily do just as much damage as the sociopath and is often just as painfully destructive in a relationship.

The narcissist may be hardworking, high-functioning, outgoing, exhibitionistic, and very vocal in his exaggerated sense of self-importance—*or* he may appear fragile and be socially isolated (to avoid reminders of his lack of importance in the real world, and to make it possible to dwell undisturbed on his thoughts of being better than other human beings). The sociopath is seldom committed to any achievement except manipulation and domination, and he certainly is not happy with simply being left alone to nurture his thoughts.

In general, the narcissist delights in being singled out; the sociopath wishes to blend in.

The narcissist is likely to be drawn toward recognition and celebrity, the sociopath toward control and actual power. The narcissist lives to be admired; the sociopath does not necessarily need to be admired, unless gaining admiration facilitates his control of other people.

The narcissist notoriously "flips," often suddenly, between seeing someone as all good and seeing that same individual as all bad. The sociopath does not much concern himself with whether other individuals are good or bad; he sees them only as game pieces. He may drop a relationship abruptly, but only because he has decided that an individual is no longer rewarding in the context of his game and therefore no longer deserving of his attention, not because he has changed his mind about that individual's true nature.

In the final analysis the difference is, once again, warmth versus coldness. The narcissist has a conscience, can feel warmly toward family and friends, can certainly love his children. (Very destructively for his children, however, he may not completely recognize them as people who are separate from himself.) This difference—a rudimentary ability to connect and love, versus the cold absence of this ability—is why the sociopath cannot be helped and the narcissist occasionally can be, and this is obviously an important consideration. The sociopath will enter therapy only if he is court-ordered, or perhaps if there is some other motivating contingency—one that has, of course, nothing to do with the pursuit of psychological change—and will depart as soon as possible. The narcissist, in contrast, sometimes attends therapy voluntarily and may stay for a while—because he is in real pain, usually over the inexplicable (to him) loss of a relationship, or of several relationships.

THE CHILL FACTOR AND THE PITY PLAY

If you remember only two specific characteristics in forming your differential diagnosis between sociopathy and narcissism, let it be these:

1. *Sociopathy is all about the thrill of coldly "playing" with people the way a predator plays with its prey.* A narcissist unintentionally damages other people's lives, often severely, but he or she is not a coldly calculating predator who torments people for the fun of it. A narcissist is not ice-cold. A sociopath is.

2. *Sociopaths are far more skilled than narcissists—or anyone else—in the art of the "pity play."* The narcissist may be

hypochondriacal (actually believing she or he has nonexistent medical problems), but seldom engages in intentional pity plays. Indeed, narcissists, with their need to feel superior, are strongly opposed to appearing pitiful.

This story details the sociopathic victimization of a young man's friend:

I'm still in a state of disbelief about Jim, a man my roommate, Kevin, started a friendship with. He invited Jim to live with us within a week, without consulting me. Kevin has a compassionate nature, and as it turned out, that was what mattered most to Jim.

A lot of what Jim said seemed to have no purpose other than to shock us. He told us that his older brother was in jail for life because he murdered his own grandfather. He said that he was writing a novel for a big New York City publisher for which he would soon receive a hundred-thousand-dollar advance. He went so far as to say he would be going on a book tour and doing the talk-show circuit. He even claimed that he had recovered from Stage 4 colon cancer a few years ago. On a few occasions when we had other people over, he'd suck praise and sympathy out of them with his tales.

Even after we knew that Jim was a chronic liar, Kevin found it hard to let go. He felt sorry for Jim and assumed that his parents had done a number on him to make him so desperate for attention. But at last Kevin realized that we could no longer have Jim living with us. After Kevin told him he had to go, Jim told us to go screw ourselves. That was two years ago, and we haven't heard from him since. I often wonder if he latched on to someone else and just keeps repeating this scenario.

From a cold psychological distance, the sociopathic Jim watched as people reacted to his phony tales—conscience-bound people who were unlikely to suspect that anyone would lie about such things. He pulled the strings of those around him by taking advantage of an integral and healthy aspect of them that had never been part of his own constricted emotional makeup: the ability to bond. It was not that narcissism prevented him from understanding his effect on these people. It was that he simply did not care.

EIGHT

SOCIOPATHY AT THE INSTITUTIONAL LEVEL

Corporations and Governments

"Everywhere there is one principle of justice, which is the interest of the stronger."

—PLATO, *The Republic*

Throughout the book I have been speaking of sociopaths as individuals. But except in its neurological aspect, consciencelessness is not restricted to individuals. Groups, institutions, corporations, and governments can also behave sociopathically.

Having the capacity to identify individuals who are prone to sociopathy before they wreak havoc would be invaluable. With this in mind, the legal system has turned to mental health experts, hoping they can provide a way to sort individual criminals who have a conscience from those who do not. Robert Hare's Psychopathy Checklist is a diagnostic tool and highly regarded research aid that in recent years has been adopted eagerly by the criminal justice system, primarily to assess the likelihood of future violence in individual criminals and the possibility (or not) of rehabilitation. The twenty items on the PCL-R assess lifestyle and criminal behavior and characteristics such as glib and superficial charm, grandiosity, need for stimulation, pathological lying, conning and manipulating, lack of remorse, callousness, poor behavioral controls, impulsivity, irresponsibility, and failure to accept responsibility for one's own actions. Each of the items is scored on a three-point scale (0, 1, 2), according to specific criteria that are evaluated using a semi-structured interview, the individual's file, and collateral information. The checklist has a maximum total score of 40, and conventionally a score of 30 or more is thought to identify a "psychopath," for whom the likelihood of rehabilitation is slim.

Overall, research indicates that under adequate conditions the Hare Psychopathy Checklist can be reliably scored, and that it does have some value in estimating the probability of future crime and violence, particularly in the population of adult, white, male offenders with which the test was originally developed. However, questions remain concerning the test's inter-rater reliability in forensic situations and its validity when applied to understudied populations (women and ethnic minorities). Research continues on these important issues.

And what do we do when the sociopath is not an individual but a group—a corporation or a government?

SOCIOPATHIC CORPORATIONS

As University of British Columbia law professor Joel Bakan writes in *The Corporation: The Pathological Pursuit of Profit and Power*, the modern corporation is "singularly self-interested and unable to feel genuine concern for others in any context." He points out that, as a legal entity, a corporation is actually mandated to serve one and only one goal: to generate profits for its shareholders. In effect, the corporation has no legal or moral obligation to consider the welfare of workers, people in general, or the environment. Indeed, its role as profit maximizer may require it to ride roughshod over, subvert, or ignore obstructive considerations such as morality and the safety and happiness of human beings. Sound familiar? Most people would find this "personality" sociopathic in a human, yet it has often been accepted in the business sphere.

Of course, corporations are supposed to make money and listen to feedback from the stockholders. But if nothing stands in their way, the trajectory toward sociopathy can gain steam. A corporation need not be run by sociopaths to exhibit sociopathic tendencies. It can be relentlessly destructive and coldly irresponsible even if headed by psychologically normal CEOs who go home every night and behave lovingly and responsibly toward their families and friends. Over time, corporate executives may gradually lower the bar on their ethics as opportunities for greater earnings appear. Eventually, this attitude can become the de facto ethos of the entire organization. The employees may not even recognize that they are jeopardizing the public they claim to serve.

Bakan states that the corporation "remains, as it was at the time of its origins as a modern business institution in the middle of the nineteenth century, a legally designated 'person' designed to valorize self-interest and invalidate moral concern." He adds, "Only pragmatic concerns for its own interests and the laws of the land constrain the corporation's predatory instincts, and often that is not enough to stop it from destroying lives, damaging communities, and endangering the planet as a whole." In other words, if corporations are "persons," they are conscienceless persons, motivated exclusively by the bottom line.

Exposés of corporations sacrificing the well-being of customers to this bottom line have been the subject of many newspaper columns and lawsuits in recent years. The behavior of these companies vividly demonstrates how ethics were sidestepped to the point where heightened risk of illness, injury, or even death became part of the equation—an acceptable cost of doing business.

A prime example of corporation as sociopath: Monsanto. This company started shifting away from integrity in the 1920s with its introduction of PCBs, which were banned by the EPA in the 1970s. A number of documents show that Monsanto knew about the health hazards of these substances—as well as those of Agent Orange, the herbicide used in the Vietnam War that it produced in partnership with the Dow Chemical Company. Estimates show that Agent Orange was responsible for half a million deaths and an equal number of babies born with birth defects. Court documents revealed that Monsanto knew of but did not publicize these potentially deadly effects when it sold Agent Orange to the government.

More recently, the pesticide Roundup, also produced by

Monsanto, has come under the gun. Research has shown that its main ingredient, glyphosate, may be carcinogenic—a finding that Monsanto has worked hard to discredit. Internal Monsanto emails show that the company continually rejected the research and warnings of independent experts about the dangers of its product. After one genotoxicity expert raised concern about Roundup's potential impact on humans, for example, Monsanto's response was to seek another expert and issue a press release stating the product posed no risks.

Some of the most disturbing sociopathic behavior has been commonplace in an industry that purports to protect human health: pharmaceutical companies. They typically fund their own research and pay doctors hefty sums to showcase favorable data and, at medical conferences and symposia, downplay less favorable data. Lawsuits involving payments in the billions of dollars attest to the sociopathy of companies that have willfully buried data and sugarcoated the profiles of drugs to expand market share.

One of the most dire public health crises in the country today stems in part from behavior by pharmaceutical companies that turned painkillers into agonizing addiction and death. Opioid addiction has been declared a public health emergency and was responsible for some 47,000 overdose deaths in the United States in 2017 alone. Purdue Pharma, which produces OxyContin, downplayed the addiction risks of this drug while urging doctors to prescribe at high doses to maximize profits. Tragically, as prescriptions of OxyContin rose, so did addiction and drug-related deaths.

Mounting evidence of unethical marketing practices resulted

in litigation against the company. In 2007, Purdue and the company's top three executives had to pay $634.5 million in fines after pleading guilty to misrepresenting the dangers of OxyContin. More recently, it has come to light that McKinsey & Company, Purdue Pharma's consulting company, offered advice on how to "turbocharge" sales of OxyContin, block efforts to reduce opioid use—and even downplay the emotional laments of mothers of teenagers who had overdosed on the drug. Purdue apparently had no qualms about following these recommendations, putting profits ahead of human lives.

Minimizing the dangers of drugs, unfortunately, has often been part of the strategy for promoting them. This has been well documented in companies that produce antidepressants. A reassessment of published research on Paxil, a GlaxoSmithKline (GSK) product, found that the drug had not been shown to perform better than placebo when studied. Even worse, data on heightened suicide risk for adolescents taking the drug remained largely hidden.

Pharmaceutical companies can provide products that also can improve health and save lives. Quite the opposite can be said for tobacco manufacturers, which have gone to great lengths to retain and increase their customer base of smokers. Although cigarette smoking among adults in the United States has declined by more than 50 percent since 1964, it still kills nearly half a million Americans a year.

When a report by the Surgeon General in 1964 linked cigarette smoking to lung cancer and heart disease, the tobacco industry responded by claiming there was no scientific evidence that smoking endangered health. It held to this claim even though the report was based on more than seven thousand articles related to smoking and disease. Until fairly recently, Big Tobacco continued to maintain that cigarette smoking is not addictive. Yet internal documents have revealed that they saw chemical dependence as the key to holding on to their market, and that they knew nicotine posed health risks. These documents revealed also that tobacco company employees were specifically instructed not to publish or circulate findings on the health risks of smoking.

While cigarettes can kill people over time, it takes only a moment for an unsafe automobile to maim or kill. In the 1970s, it was learned that the Ford Pinto had a defective fuel system that increased the risk of the car exploding upon impact. Ford knew of a design change that could reduce this risk, but the company rejected it based on a risk/benefit analysis showing that the new design would result in 180 fewer deaths but cost $11 per car. Overall, the cost of the design change would be $137 million, versus an estimated $49.5 million for deaths, injuries, and car damage without the design change. (Yes, the company came up with a monetary figure for each human death and injury.) Ford justified rejecting the new design by claiming that its financial cost was greater than its benefit to society. Concern for the welfare of consumers seemed not to register with them. Accident victims sued and won huge settlements from the conscienceless car company.

It is heartening that people who honor human connection and responsibility are more likely to take action against corporate transgression today. A number of high-profile lawsuits have successfully challenged the disreputable practices of pharmaceutical companies, car companies, and a host of other corporations. As Bakan states, "The scandals have arrived, and people's distrust of corporations is running high, perhaps as high as it did during the Great Depression."

A profit motive gone wild seems to have turned certain industries into sociopathic institutions. But steps can be taken to reverse this awful trend. Bakan suggests several ways in which the ruthlessness of corporations might be curbed: staffing enforcement agencies at realistic levels, setting fines high enough to deter wealthy corporations from committing crimes, increasing the liability of those at the top for their corporation's illegal behaviors, barring repeat offenders from government contracts, and suspending the charters of corporations that persistently exploit and harm the public. The sad truth is that corporations will get away with this behavior if possible. The goal is to stop making it possible.

What makes seemingly upright people serve as allies in a sociopathic cause as a corporation or country veers to the dark side? The famous Stanley Milgram studies on obedience to authority showed that at least six out of ten people will follow the orders of a perceived authority figure when in his presence. This held true even when the authority figures were in direct defiance of the strongest prohibitions of conscience—commands including those that asked participants to harm other human beings they did not know.

In this experiment, two men were assigned to be either a "teacher" or "learner." In a separate room, the learner was strapped to a chair and had an electrode attached to his wrist. He was told that he must learn a list of word pairs (blue box, nice day, wild duck, etc.), and that whenever he made a mistake, he would receive an electric shock. (The learner was actually an actor and received no electric shocks during the test.) The teacher's assignment was to conduct the test and deliver the shocks, increasing the voltage with each new wrong response. During the testing, an experimenter stood behind the teacher. As shouts of pain and expressions of desperation escalated with the supposed increases in voltage, the experimenter told the teacher to continue. The result: twenty-six of Milgram's original forty subjects kept shocking the learner up to the highest voltage level, even after he asked to be released from the experiment. A subsequent study with women had similar results.

The oft-replicated outcome of his obedience study led Milgram to make a pronouncement that has haunted, and also motivated, students of human nature: "A substantial proportion of people will do what they are told to do, irrespective of the content of the act and without limitations of conscience, so long as they perceive that the command comes from a legitimate authority." Milgram believed that authority could put conscience to sleep because the obedient person makes an "adjustment of thought," which is to see himself *as not responsible for his own actions*.

SOCIOPATHIC GOVERNMENTS

In some circumstances, evil acts and the pain that attends them can result from the mere nearness of sociopathy. In times of war, in prisons, and in the context of deeply rooted ethnic hatred and even ordinary fear-driven bigotry, we subvert our consciences using *moral exclusion*. This term was coined by Ervin Staub in *The Roots of Evil: The Origins of Genocide and Other Group Violence* to describe the psychological process by which a person or group is seen as undeserving of the humane treatment morally mandated for everyone else. This view sees others as "its" rather than as people. Behavior toward them is not bound by conscience, which is a feeling of obligation toward our fellow human beings. All too often, people have been incited by the ruthless and the powerful to engage in moral exclusion of the out-group or the "enemy."

In *moral inversion*, an "evil" situation is convincingly redefined as good. Public administration ethicists Guy Adams and Danny Balfour explain: "Ordinary people may simply be acting appropriately in their organizational role, just doing what is expected of them while participating in what a critical observer (usually well after the fact) would call evil. Under conditions of what we term moral inversion, ordinary people can engage in acts of administrative evil while believing that what they are doing is not only procedurally correct but, in fact, good."

Like sociopathic evil, administrative evil is hard to pin down. Adams and Balfour write, "Because administrative evil is typically masked, no one has to accept an overt invitation to commit an evil act, because such overt invitations are almost never made. Rather, it may come in the form of an expert or technical role, couched in appropriate language, or it may even come packaged as a good and worthy project (moral inversion)." As moral exclusion sabotages our sense of conscience, moral inversion blinds our ability to be empathic toward those who may be harmed by our actions.

Evil acts may become acceptable to those under the sway of sociopaths in positions of authority, because we are capable of reacting with moral exclusion, hatred, and bigotry; and because of our involvement in systems from which, due to greed or just plain-vanilla psychological denial, human interrelatedness and conscience have been scooped out like the vital but messy seed-heart of a melon. Whether enacted by profoundly disordered people, ordinary people under their sway, or destructive corporations or governments, evil is the product of an absence, a hollowness where connectedness, empathy, and conscience should be.

We've seen what can happen in corporations. This evil presents a greater threat when it occurs in government, since so many more people may be affected by government policy. We hear reports nearly every week of yet another personal or financial scandal in our government. We watch as Congress remains mired in a quicksand of infighting and fear politics and begin to wonder out loud whether perhaps parts of our government have devolved into assemblies of titular leaders whose only genuine objective is to hang on to the reins of power. From other parts of the world, we hear accusations of imperialism and, if domination is the national agenda, we wonder who chose it, when, and why. If there is any positive feature of this situation, it is that our society has begun to understand that the *character* of a leader—the degree to which he or she feels connected to other human beings and is empathic, responsible, and honest—is supremely important. Increasingly, we look for moral leaders in government, and we pay attention to signs of antisocial ones—chronic lying, a lack of empathy, and a pattern of placing a power agenda ahead of the good of the people.

You will recall from the last chapter that, if pressed, I would be inclined to place someone who behaves as President Trump does in the category of narcissism. But history—the twentieth century alone—has given us no shortage of dictators who cast a sociopathic shadow over their nations and subject their people to policies that mandate tremendous suffering. The name that probably comes to mind first in this category is Adolf Hitler. Unlike other dictators who have targeted only their enemies in ruthless purges, Hitler attempted to wipe out an entire religion. He used moral exclusion to justify his militaristic ambitions, claiming that the countries of Eastern Europe were populated by "inferior" people and therefore Germany had the right to annex them.

Lying was a key component of Hitler's propaganda, and it facilitated deception on a massive scale. He had discovered an important principle of sidestepping the truth: big lies often are more effective than little ones. His God-like vision of himself, combined with his paranoia, allowed him to think that all of his thoughts and behaviors were inviolate, while compelling him to purge any potential threats to his power. Meanwhile, he surrounded himself with sycophants who were infected by his rabid nationalism. Thus the sociopathic regime was sustained.

When we consider the career of Joseph Stalin, parallels with Hitler emerge. He, too, was extremely paranoid and had a deep sense of inferiority. He would vehemently reject any ideas that did not agree with his, and even a psychiatrist's diagnosis of him as paranoiac could not stick; he declared that his own personality was not an issue regarding his ability to govern. When Stalin's policies failed, he would come up with explanations that did not threaten their validity and assign blame to whomever he could. He controlled through fear—fear of death, fear of torture, fear of exile—and further consolidated his power by denying there was a God, thus eliminating any thought of power above his own.

Mao Tse-tung was among the worst of the dictator sociopaths, overcome by his own sense of power and absolute lack of concern for human suffering. By inducing fear and through sheer force of personality, Mao managed to promote policies that devastated the country but were largely useless. He would accuse anyone who objected to his plan for rapid advancement of being counterrevolutionary—a stance reminiscent of Stalin's rationale for exterminating naysayers. His Great Leap Forward, a program that he claimed would make China the leading grain producer in the world, resulted in government storehouses overflowing with grain at the expense of millions of starving Chinese farmers. This clear introduction of moral inversion brought disaster to the country.

Pol Pot's reign of terror with the Khmer Rouge in Cambodia was in a way even more egregious than what happened under Hitler, Stalin, or Mao. In just four years during the late 1970s, the policies of that government may have resulted in more than three million deaths, according to some estimates. Pol Pot's lack of concern for human life was embodied by the slogan of the Khmer Rouge: "Keeping you is no profit; losing you is no loss." The merging of his supreme ego with his immorality birthed savage tactics to achieve his grand design for making Cambodia more powerful. The Khmer Rouge controlled virtually all aspects of a person's life. It became a crime to own property or jewelry, to read books, and to practice religion. A policy of "reeducation" forced civil servants, doctors, teachers, and other professionals to become field hands. Children were removed from their families and placed into military service. Everything from choice of clothing to sexual activity was proscribed by strict rules.

Many dictators have a rather simplistic vision of governing their nations, and they are often deposed when their grandiose plans and rigid autonomy lead to disaster. Unfortunately, sometimes one despot is just replaced with another. Russia, for instance, eliminated the czar but ended up with Stalin. When a revolution does not go as planned, it opens the door to a new leader with charismatic powers who may then show his corruption and consciencelessness.

Will the human race ever evolve to a point where sociopathic dictators will no longer gain a foothold? Optimism remains difficult when one scans the world and catalogs the malicious regimes that still thrive. History itself, unfortunately, does not always teach us well enough, and atrocities of the past may be "disarmed" or even denied by revisionists. In China, for example, there have been great efforts to uphold Mao's reputation. Historians there have maintained that the number of deaths attributed to Mao's policies has been "inflated by bad statistical work." Sun Jingxian, a mathematician at Shandong University and Jiangsu Normal University, claimed that famine killed just 3.66 million people during the Great Leap Forward. His claim "contradicts almost every other serious effort at accounting for the effects of Mao's changes," which put the number in the tens of millions. Other attempts to refute the scope or the very existence of notorious tragedies include Holocaust deniers. The Internet makes it easier than ever for fringe groups to mobilize with like-minded others and spread lies.

Understanding sociopathy can teach us that, at those times when we focus only on ourselves and our group and ignore our intrinsic ties to others—when we turn a blind eye to the importance of everyone's well-being—even those of us who do have conscience begin to lose our way, and the shadow of evil looms closer. Goodness lies in sensing our bonds with others; evil happens when, for whatever reasons, those feelings are numbed. Just as we regulate ourselves as individuals against our more selfish impulses, we must learn to regulate humankind as a whole. This is a tall order. It is also the only real choice we have.

It is interesting to speculate about a perhaps not-too-distant future in which we have at last developed a fully valid and reliable test for consciencelessness that goes beyond Robert Hare's Psychopathy Checklist, a future in which we are as adamant about seeing political candidates' scores on that test as we are about the disclosure of their income tax returns. How might society change if there were such a tool? Or, even more dizzying to think about, how might human history have been different had there been such a resource long ago?

NINE

THE NATURE OF GOOD

Compassion, Forgiveness, and Freedom

"We need a moral philosophy in which the concept of love, so rarely mentioned now by philosophers, can once again be made central."

—IRIS MURDOCH, *The Sovereignty of Good*

I have filled a lot of pages defining and illustrating the nature of evil, in the service of helping you recognize it and protect yourself against the sociopath in your life. In most of this final chapter I will celebrate evil's antithesis, the extraordinary nature of good in the world and the ways in which it has been expressed that can restore our faith in people and renew our positive view of the world. Those whose lives have been pummeled by conscienceless people are especially in need of this salve.

First, let me reiterate my new definition of evil as not a being or a thing, nor a shadowy aspect of normal human nature. Rather, evil is a hole, an absence of the normal ability to connect, to love, and to experience conscience. This empty chasm has swallowed up countless individual lives and far too many chapters in our collective history. Sometimes it generates a human monster—a cold-blooded mass murderer, or a serial killer, or a power-hungry warmonger, or the mastermind of a pogrom—and sometimes it engenders "merely" a heartless Ponzi schemer, or a conscience-less false lover, or a vicious and game-playing boss. The struggle between evil and good, in all of its permutations, is humanity's oldest story and possibly its most defining one. If we are to continue to survive in this contest, as our technology and global capabilities expand beyond our imaginations, we must let go of our superstitious ideas about evil and learn to recognize the currently invisible and endlessly destructive pattern that arises from the inability to love.

As an analogy: Just as today we remain confused about the nature of evil, not so long ago, we knew almost nothing about the disease of cancer. To our eyes, people simply sickened, endured great pain, and died. For centuries, we tried to explain what we saw of cancer by attributing it to divine power, or curses, or the speaking of careless words by the victim. In the Middle Ages, the divine right of kings (the belief that kings derived their right to rule directly from the will of God) was thought to give royalty the ability to heal through touch. Only when we began to understand what cancer really is—abnormal cells that tend to proliferate in an uncontrolled way and to metastasize, rather than God's will, a curse, or a form of evil energy—could we start to search for effective treatments and, ultimately, cures.

Old Scratch, Old Nick, Lucifer, Mephistopheles, Satan, Shaitan, Iblis, Ahriman, the Dark Lord—evil is called by a long list of names. We learn about the devil in childhood, by one designation or another, and he is almost impossible to evict from our heads later on. He is infused into our literature, our familiar cultural and symbolic frameworks, and our most fundamental ideas about how life works. He has even been formally sued for his misconduct. In 1971, Gerald Mayo filed a claim before the U.S. District Court for the Western District of Pennsylvania, arguing that "Satan has on numerous occasions caused plaintiff misery and unwarranted threats, against the will of plaintiff, that Satan has placed deliberate obstacles in his path and has caused plaintiff's downfall," and has thus "deprived him of his constitutional rights." The judge remarked that there was an "unofficial account of a trial in New Hampshire" that might provide something of a precedent (a sly reference to Stephen Vincent Benét's 1937 short story "The Devil and Daniel Webster") and noted also that the case would be an unusually appropriate candidate for class action status. Still, in the end, the court refused to proceed, because the plaintiff had not provided instructions as to how the U.S. Marshal could serve process on the defendant.

The devil's lack of a proper address notwithstanding, we continue to conceive of evil as a being or a force, one that is external to ourselves. Evil may try to possess or occupy us, but it never originates in us, and the notion that the devil is somewhere out there, possessing the other guy or occupying the other group, has served to reinforce bigotry and hatred throughout the centuries. In virtually every ethnic, racial, and political armed conflict that humans have fought, the in-group is on God's side and the enemy is on the devil's—the glitch in this system being, of course, that both sides cherish the identical belief. The tragic irony is that, in battles of conquest arranged by the power-hungry and the ruthless, all people, on both sides, are pawns to the very same evil: the emptiness of those who regard war as a game of control and domination played on an especially large scale. Learning about sociopathy encourages an understanding that evil is not a being or a force, but rather a tragic deficiency—an absence that sometimes occurs in the human brain and psyche—and that those afflicted with this deficiency do not all reside out there somewhere, but right here among us as well.

It is interesting to note that, in wolf packs, individual wolves who show no "pack sense" (wolves who exhibit "antisocial" behaviors) are often banished to the periphery of the pack. And there is evidence from anthropology that, in the past, human beings living in small, isolated groups sometimes dealt with the problem of sociopathy in ways that were straightforward and summary. For instance, psychiatric anthropologist Jane M. Murphy describes the Inuit concept of *kunlangeta,* which refers to a person whose "mind knows what to do but does not do it." Murphy writes that in northwest Alaska, *kunlangeta* "might be applied to a man who, for example, repeatedly lies and cheats and steals things and does not go hunting, and, when the other men are out of the village, takes sexual advantage of many women." The Inuits assume that *kunlangeta* is incurable, and so the traditional Inuit approach to such a man was to insist that he go hunting, and then, in the absence of witnesses, push him off the edge of the ice.

We no longer live in communities so small that we can reach unanimous agreement regarding the nature of each individual's character, or so isolated that every citizen will agree to share in the responsibility for a murderous group ambush. In the large and ever-shifting communities where most of us now reside, the methods used by small tribal groups can no longer resolve the thorny predicament raised by the existence of individuals who have no "pack sense." In his book *Tribe: On Homecoming and Belonging,* Sebastian Junger notes that our modern society "is a sprawling and anonymous mess where people can get away with incredible levels of dishonesty without getting caught. What tribal people would consider a profound betrayal of the group, modern society simply dismisses as fraud."

In dealing with the ancient problem of human evil (the deficit that enables the "profound betrayal" of family members, co-workers, and others with whom we normally bond), we must educate our own larger "tribe," and insist that our mental health and legal systems begin to shield and assist us. The current situation—in which individuals are left to cope on their own, without the support or even the acknowledgment of society—is often ruinous. I receive far too many accounts like the one from a father struggling with legal authorities to protect his child from a treacherously abusive ex-wife; the father was unsuccessful because a court-appointed psychologist, untrained in the manipulative charisma of sociopathy, labeled him "relationally delusional" and a "conspiracy theorist."

Slowly, our situation is changing for the better. An encouraging example of positive change, this one addressing antisocial behaviors in the workplace, is the Healthy Workplace Campaign, launched in 2002 by psychologists Ruth and Gary Namie. They point out that, except in four Canadian provinces (Québec, Saskatchewan, Ontario, and Manitoba), employers in North America face no legal repercussions when they choose to ignore internal reports of bullying in their organizations. In the United States, workers who are abused because of their membership in a protected class (race, gender, nationality, or religion, among others) can sue under civil rights laws, but our laws usually do not protect workers against viciousness perpetrated simply for the sake of viciousness.

The Healthy Workplace Campaign presses for the passage of the Healthy Workplace Bill, initially drafted by Suffolk University law professor David Yamada, which would allow any worker to sue for physical, psychological, or economic harm due to abusive treatment on the job. Workers who can demonstrate that they were subjected to hostile conduct, including verbal abuse, threats, or work sabotage, could be awarded lost wages, medical expenses, compensation for emotional distress, and punitive damages. To reassure employers who might oppose the bill, the proposed law is designed to cover only the most offensive and deliberate acts, and requires that the wrongful conduct be done with "malice" and, in most cases, that it be repeated. Also, it provides affirmative defenses (reasons the defendant should not be required to pay damages) for companies that investigate swiftly and address the problem in good faith.

The Namies emphasize that the United States is the last of the Western democracies to introduce a law forbidding "bullying-like" conduct in the workplace. The Scandinavian nations have had explicit anti-bullying laws since 1994, and many of the European Union nations have laws in place that compel employers to prevent or correct bullying. Great Britain has broad anti-harassment laws, and in 2011 Australia passed the first law that actually criminalizes workplace bullying. In the United States, the Healthy Workplace Bill has been introduced in twenty-four states and been sponsored by more than three hundred legislators.

THE POWER OF COMPASSION

Having defined "evil" as an empty hole—as the absence of conscience and the ability to love—in counterpoint, we can now identify the nature of "good." Goodness springs from our psychological completeness, our capacity to love and to feel conscience. From this place come empathy, gratitude, loyalty, and our sense of justice as well—all of the warm emotional responses that allow us to live together on this earth. We must learn to recognize, value, and protect the ability to love, which is the authentic opposite of evil. This seems simple enough, but our society, our modern "tribe," has been sabotaged by money-gathering entities with no attachment to human, cultural, or environmental well-being; the confused loyalties of our lawmakers; and a legal system that is far too easily played. For the foreseeable future, our individual lives are where we must take our stand, and where we will either start to rescue humanity or watch it begin to fade away.

When I think about this definition of "good," I often recall a message I received about an extraordinary child:

> *You probably get a lot of horrible emails about people suffering at the hands of a sociopath. My email is different. I think you will appreciate this story about compassion and morality involving a young child.*

A new kid had just moved into town. He was a bit heavy and wore thick glasses. I guess new kids often get the treatment, but this poor boy was especially ridiculed because of his appearance and squeaky voice. My son claims he didn't participate, but he admitted witnessing abuse of the boy on the playground and while walking home from their elementary school. Other kids poked at his belly with sticks and called him a beached whale, stuff like that.

One day after they had pushed the boy into a mud puddle, a girl asked my son softly, "Why does he deserve to be treated so badly?" She helped the boy up and told him that what had happened to him was not fair. The girl went over to the abusive boys and told them that they followed the rules when they were playing baseball and football, so why did they think it was okay to break the rules here? The boys shrugged and wandered off. But it was the last time they teased the new kid. My son later told me that he felt ashamed that he hadn't tried to stop the other kids from their bad behavior. I have a feeling he'd be willing to do so now.

As an example of the power of compassion to uplift the person who feels it, I offer the following excerpt from a message sent to me by another person who is especially loving and empathic. In addition to illustrating some of the positive outcomes of forgiveness, her words speak to anyone who has come to view herself as a "sociopath magnet"—a good person who seems to attract sociopaths to her life as honey draws flies, for reasons that feel maddeningly mysterious to her. The author of this message has discovered, to her surprise, that a sociopath is lured by another person's virtues:

I want to thank you so much for your book. I read it at a time when I really needed it, and it has helped me, in a way, reclaim my sense of self. I had been mired in a destructive relationship for two years. When I first met Harold, he was working as an accountant. We really hit it off. He was very funny and intelligent, and I was impressed by his deep thoughts about life. A few months after we started going out, he abruptly quit his job. It was a waste of his talents, he told me. He had been thinking about this screenplay, some science-fiction plot, for years and was now going to act on it. He was certain a studio would scoop it up and make him famous, so he couldn't let the mundane tasks of life distract him. At first I was impressed. I moved in with him and helped him put all his attention into his work by doing all the shopping, preparing all the meals, getting his car serviced. He never thanked me, but I chalked it up to him being totally immersed in his work.

Then started all the appointments with doctors. He must have seen ten different specialists in just a month, claiming he had unbearable pain. The doctors were instant quacks once they told him they found nothing wrong with him. His need for attention became overwhelming. He would scream at me if I got home from work five minutes later than usual. I asked him if I could see what he was writing and he barked at me. It was none of my business, he said. The fact that I cared about him and was doing everything for him meant nothing to him.

I learned he had been lying to me. He would often go to the library on Saturday afternoons but never took out or returned any books. One day I followed him, keeping just out of sight as he went into a café and kissed a woman who clearly had been waiting for him. I told him what I'd seen and he laughed hysterically. He said it was his agent, that there was a big deal in the works with a movie producer. The next weekend I went to the café early and saw the same woman there. I told her the situation and she started apologizing. She was a hairdresser at a local salon. Then Harold came to the café and pretended not to know either one of us!

That was the end of the relationship, which I realize in hindsight should have happened much sooner. I don't think he ever cared about me. He was unable to care about anybody.

I had lost my perspective on how to have a genuine relationship with a man. Months after it was over with Harold, I still felt in a kind of limbo from what he did to me. It made me think that I would have difficulty recognizing whether someone's feelings for me were genuine. My self-confidence had been shattered and I didn't know if I could put the pieces back together again.

Reading your book changed all that. I can see the pattern of Harold's behavior for what it is, and my positive traits were what attracted him to me. It was the goodness of my heart that made him latch on. I recognize again that I have worth for just who I am. My willingness to totally be there for someone in need was actually a good thing. Recognizing this has also allowed me to forgive Harold, since he is what he is and can't be any

*different. So thank you for making me be better able to
recognize my virtues and reclaim my trust in myself.*

Compassion and forgiveness open the door to freedom, and
to the rest of your life. The alternatives—continued hatred and a
desire for revenge—are traps that can imprison you for a very
long time, if you let them. Picture hatred as an ugly spiked this-
tle, one that will eventually grow taller than you are, sending out
surreptitious poisonous vines that twine and tangle around you,
head to toe, until you are stuck where you stand. Hatred can
easily do just as much damage to your life as a sociopath. The
lust for revenge will seduce you into using other people in the
service of its demands. It will pollute your good relationships and
waste years of your life.

Unless we proceed with sufficient knowledge, awareness, and
compassion, we are (ironically) in danger of applying moral exclusion to the offensive and frightening minority of people called
"sociopaths." Especially since we will one day be able to diagnose
the very young, a turn to the moral exclusion of the people who
are the subject of this book would inevitably lead to destructive
choices on our part, blindly ruinous of other lives and also of our
own hearts. Sociopaths remain human beings, and perceiving
them as hardly even human is just as insidious as the moral exclusion of any other group of people. Standing your ground
against cold, abusive behavior works better and actually *feels better* when done calmly and minus the fantasy of revenge.

In the future, perhaps we will create neurological techniques
to grant the potential for full paralimbic development to the

brains of babies born without that potential, and therefore without the capacity to develop conscience. We may be able to approach the neurological problem of sociopathy with a degree of clinical immediacy and aplomb similar to that with which we approach the correction of the heart in "blue baby syndrome" (Fallot's syndrome) and other congenital defects, and joyously invite formerly neurologically stunted infants to join us in a world where love is possible.

I should specify that forgiving is not at all the same as forgetting. *Forgiving* can liberate you. In contrast, simply *forgetting* what you have learned about someone through painful experience is naive, dangerous, and unnecessary. Sometimes compassion and forgiving are better done from a distance, and there is nothing psychologically or spiritually wrong with being rational and using the information you have gathered about a ruthless person to protect yourself and the other people in your life. To forgive is not to forget. Indeed, forgiving something that is mostly forgotten is not real forgiveness.

POSITIVE PSYCHOLOGY

Beginning with the visionary work and influence of Martin Seligman, the entire discipline of psychology has taken a new and thrilling direction, away from its preoccupation with that which makes us miserable (or, at best, adapted to misery) and toward the study of happiness, character, and meaning—a psychology of positive human functioning. The paradigm-shattering discipline fathered by Seligman is called *positive psychology,* and perhaps the dominant finding to emerge from research in this new field is that our happiness is determined largely by the quantity and quality of our interpersonal connections. Thanks to this research, the responses that foster our bonds with each other, those of empathy, compassion, altruism, love—and yes, forgiveness—are scientifically shown to be associated with personal happiness and meaning.

Mind you, unless you are a gentle Buddhist master or a gifted monk, I will not suggest that you actually learn to love the sociopath who has targeted you. This may be more than you believe you can tolerate. However, I do recommend that you develop a certain compassion for this damaging person who has crossed your path. There is a hollow space in his heart, so to speak. He will not ever be able to experience love—not for anyone, not even his children. He is deficient in a long list of other ways as well, and ultimately self-destructive. Though he may think of himself as superior to all of us who are "limited" by conscience—and, for a while, he may convince his victims of his preeminence—in reality his life is dry, endlessly monotonous, and tragically empty of meaning.

Love is a great deal more than social glue. If our compelling sense of connectedness, our conscience, evolved as a way to promote our survival by keeping us in groups where we could be stronger than we were as individuals, then it has worked very well and hopefully will continue to do so. But, more wonderful still, somewhere in the yawning chasms of imponderable time, attachment—love—turned into something greater, something that at its strongest can cause a person to relinquish her own safety, and life itself, for someone else. The emotional facility of normal human beings is now so powerful that we can keep a deceased person we have deeply loved, and who has loved us, alive in our hearts to our own death.

With enough love, not only can we remember a boundless number of small details from the past—a crooked smile, a figure of speech—we can also postdict the nuances of what that person would say and do in any particular situation in the present, every preference he or she would express right now, every aversion, every value. For us to feel the existence of people we have truly loved, their physical presence, though we may ache for it, is no longer required.

So the planet dances with the known billions of us who are alive today, and just as electrically with the energies of countless billions whose biological lives have ended. Emotional attachment, in the course of time, has evolved past its role as a mere guardian of the survival of mortal creatures. The emotions that link us with each other have transcended themselves, and love contains the seed of eternity.

Helplessly, and quite independent of religious faith, it is our nature to long for the individual embodiment of life. We do not do well with intangible stand-ins. And we are afflicted with fear by the inescapability of our own death, the certain dissolution of our familiar bodies, the prospect of an end to the parade of thoughts and pictures in our own minds—the mental panoply that began in a corporal nothingness we cannot recall. But the true things that happen in our lives, and all that have happened in the past to anyone who has ever lived, will always be true. We did it: life transcended itself by love.

Forged by the eons and infinitely more precious than any material thing, this triumph, our ability to love, to bond, to be empathic—and, yes, to feel guilty when we hurt someone—deserves to be honored and acted upon. From the modest means of the little helper chimpanzee in his feeding tree to the heights of effectiveness we can achieve with our large human brains, the resources of living things are best spent not in the pursuit of power—or of revenge—but in the service of our interconnectedness. This is an ancient contest—a minority of sociopathic predators versus a majority of loving protectors—a struggle we can and must win.

Fortunately, our own power is inestimably greater than the sociopath's, because it is not generated by a pathological hunger for control, not enabled by an emotional vacuum. Rather, our power is based in emotional wholeness, our ability to love and to bond steadfastly with each other, to have one another's backs. (And, quite simply, there are more of us than there are of them.) We must use our power to save ourselves, those we love, and the planet. We have the power, and we have a mission. And when the sociopath cannot be avoided, we should—and *can*—outsmart him.

Largely overlooked by our society at present, the job of championing relationship and conscience tends to fall to us as individuals, in our personal and work lives, and in our lives as parents: a sociopath finally must be confronted, and taken on without losing sight of our own humanity. The task is sometimes terrifying and nearly always isolating, but when sociopathy cannot be avoided, the courageous and compassionate individual who stands against it elevates us all.

NOTES

ONE. A HOLE IN THE PSYCHE:
UNDERSTANDING SOCIOPATHY

page 19   **the so-called bible of psychiatric disorders:** American Psychiatric Association, *Diagnostic and Statistical Manual of Mental Disorders,* 5th ed. (Washington, DC: American Psychiatric Association, 2013). For a thoroughgoing critique of the development of the *DSMs,* see Gary Greenberg, *The Book of Woe: The DSM and the Unmaking of Psychiatry* (New York: Plume, 2013), and my review of that book, "The Pernicious Politics of the DSM-V," *The New Republic,* May 8, 2013.

page 25   **only about 20 percent of prison inmates in the United States:** See R. Hare, K. Strachan, and A. Forth, "Psychopathy and Crime: A Review," in *Clinical Approaches to Mentally Disordered Offenders,* ed. Kevin Howells and Clive Hollin (New York: Wiley, 1993); and S. Hart and R. Hare, "Psychopathy: Assessment and Association with Criminal Conduct," in *Handbook of Antisocial Behavior,* ed. D. Stoff, J. Breiling, and J. Maser (New York: Wiley, 1997).

page 25   **contains a disproportionate number of chronic offenders:** S. A. Mednick, L. Kirkegaard-Sorense, B. Hutchings, et al. (1977), "An example of biosocial interaction research: The interplay of socioenvironmental and individual factors in the etiology of criminal behavior," in *Biosocial Bases of Criminal Behavior,* ed. Sarnoff A. Mednick and Karl O. Christiansen (New York: Gardner Press, 1978).

page 25   **able to deceive and manipulate judges and parole boards:** S. Porter, M. Woodworth, and A. R. Birt (2000), "Truth, lies, and videotape: An investigation of the ability of federal parole officers to detect deception," *Law and Human Behavior* 24(6): 643–58.

page 25   **"Academy Award–winning performances":** Stephen Porter, BBC News, February 19, 2009, http://news.bbc.co.uk/go/pr/fr/-/2/hi/health /7833672.stm, published 2009/02/09 12:16:24 GMT.

TWO. WHEN THE SOCIOPATH BELONGS TO YOU:
CHILDREN WITHOUT CONSCIENCE

page 44   **Conduct disorder can be diagnosed:** R. C. Kessler, P. Berglund, O. Demler, et al. (2005), "Lifetime Prevalence and Age-of-Onset Distributions of *DSM-IV* Disorders in the National Comorbidity Survey Replication," *Archives of General Psychiatry* 62(7): 593–602 (nationally representative face-to-face household survey conducted between February 2001 and April 2003, using the fully structured World Health Organization World Mental Health Survey version of the Composite International Diagnostic Interview); D. G. V. Mitchell, R. A. Richell, A. Leonard, R. Blair, and R. James (2006), "Emotion at the expense of cognition: Psychopathic individuals outperform controls on an operant response task," *Journal of Abnormal Psychology* 115(3): 559–66. For a detailed discussion of the heritability of the neurological basis of sociopathy, see Martha Stout, *The Sociopath Next Door* (New York: Broadway Books, 2005), 120–24.

page 45   **60 percent of individuals diagnosed:** E. Viding and H. Larsson (2007), "Aetiology of antisocial behavior," *International Congress Series*

1304(1): 121–32. On conduct disorder turning into antisocial personality disorder: B. B. Lahey, R. Loeber, J. D. Burke, and B. Applegate (2005), "Predicting future antisocial personality disorder in males from a clinical assessment in childhood," *Journal of Consulting and Clinical Psychology* 73(3): 389–99.

page 46 **In an extensive review of the research:** P. J. Frick and S. F. White (2008), "Research review: The importance of callous-unemotional traits for developmental models of aggressive and antisocial behavior," *Journal of Child Psychology and Psychiatry* 49(4): 359–75. The quote is on page 359.

page 47 **Frick and other experts have maintained:** For more about this argument, see the following: R. E. Kahn, P. J. Frick, E. Youngstrom, et al. (2012), "The effects of including a callous-unemotional specifier for the diagnosis of conduct disorder," *Journal of Child Psychology and Psychiatry* 53(3): 271–82; R. Rowe, B. Maughan, P. Moran, et al. (2010), "The role of callous and unemotional traits in the diagnosis of conduct disorder," *Journal of Child Psychology and Psychiatry* 51(6): 688–95; F. E. Scheepers, J. K. Buitelaar, and W. Matthys (2011), "Conduct Disorder and the specifier callous and unemotional traits in the *DSM-5*," *European Child and Adolescent Psychiatry* 20(2): 89–93; P. J. Frick (2009), "Extending the construct of psychopathy to youth: Implications for understanding, diagnosing, and treating antisocial children and adolescents," *Canadian Journal of Psychiatry* 54(12): 803–12.

page 47 **report published in 2012 in the United Kingdom:** E. Viding, N. M. G. Fontaine, and E. J. McCrory (2012), "Antisocial behaviour in children with and without callous-unemotional traits," *Journal of the Royal Society of Medicine* 105(5): 195–200. Those interested in methodologies used to research the possible genetic link in conduct disorder children with callous-unemotional traits may wish to refer to these two early studies: E. Viding, N. M. G. Fontaine, B. R. Oliver, and R. Plomin (2009), "Negative parental discipline, conduct problems and callous-unemotional traits: Monozygotic twin differences study," *British Journal of Psychiatry* 195(5): 414–19; and E. Viding, A. P. Jones, P. J. Frick, et al. (2008), "Heritability of antisocial behaviour at 9: Do callous-unemotional traits matter?" *Developmental Science* 11(1): 17–22.

page 47   **early exposure to lead:** K. M. Cecil, C. J. Brubaker, C. M. Adler, et al. (2008), "Decreased Brain Volume in Adults with Childhood Lead Exposure," *PLOS Medicine* 5(5): e112, https://doi.org/10.1371/journal .pmed.0050112.

page 48   **In 1994, a study was published:** B. K. Luntz and C. S. Widom (1994), "Antisocial personality disorder in abused and neglected children grown up," *American Journal of Psychiatry* 151(5): 670–74.

page 49   **In 2010, researchers:** A. Raine, L. Lee, Y. Yang, and P. Colletti (2010), "Neurodevelopmental marker for limbic maldevelopment in antisocial personality disorder and psychopathy," *British Journal of Psychiatry* 197(3): 186–92.

page 51   **When faced in the laboratory with tasks involving emotional language:** S. Williamson, T. J. Harpur, and R. D. Hare (1991), "Abnormal processing of affective words by psychopaths," *Psychophysiology* 28(3): 260–73; B. R. Loney, P. J. Frick, C. B. Clements, et al. (2003), "Callous-unemotional traits, impulsivity, and emotional processing in adolescents with antisocial behavior problems," *Journal of Clinical Child and Adolescent Psychology* 32(1): 66–80.

page 51   **Sociopathic adults also do not show the same pattern of startle responses:** G. K. Levenston, C. J. Patrick, M. M. Bradley, and P. J. Lang (2000), "The psychopath as observer: Emotion and attention in picture processing," *Journal of Abnormal Psychology* 109(3): 373–85; S. K. Sutton, J. E. Vitale, and J. P. Newman (2002), "Emotion among women with psychopathy during picture perception," *Journal of Abnormal Psychology* 111(4): 610–19.

page 51   **Laboratory tests using simple tasks:** D. G. Mitchell, R. A. Richell, A. Leonard, and R. J. R. Blair (2006), "Emotion at the expense of cognition: Psychopathic individuals outperform controls on an operant response task," *Journal of Abnormal Psychology* 115(3): 559–66.

page 51   **deficits in recognizing facial displays of emotion:** A. A. Marsh and

R. J. R. Blair (2008), "Deficits in facial affect recognition among antisocial populations: A meta-analysis," *Neuroscience and Biobehavioral Reviews* 32(3): 454–65.

page 51   **sociopaths suffer from a dysfunction in the amygdala:** James Blair, Derek Mitchell, and Karina Blair, *The Psychopath: Emotion and the Brain* (Hoboken, NJ: Wiley-Blackwell, 2005); K. A. Kiehl (2006), "A cognitive neuroscience perspective on psychopathy: Evidence for paralimbic system dysfunction," *Psychiatry Research* 142(2–3): 107–28; R. J. R. Blair (2005), "Applying a cognitive neuroscience perspective to the disorder of psychopathy," *Development and Psychopathology* 17(3): 865–91; K. A. Kiehl; A. T. Bates, K. R. Laurens, et al. (2006), "Brain potentials implicate temporal lobe abnormalities in criminal psychopaths," *Journal of Abnormal Psychology* 115(3): 443–53.

page 51   ***increased* activation in the dorsolateral region of the prefrontal cortex:** H. L. Gordon, A. A. Baird, and A. End (2004), "Functional differences among those high and low on a trait measure of psychopathy," *Biological Psychiatry* 56(7): 516–21; J. Intrator, R. D. Hare, P. Stritzke, et al. (1997), "A brain imaging (single photon emission computerized tomography) study of semantic and affective processing in psychopaths," *Biological Psychiatry* 42(2): 96–103; K. A. Kiehl, A. M. Smith, R. D. Hare, et al. (2001), "Limbic abnormalities in affective processing by criminal psychopaths as revealed by functional magnetic resonance imaging," *Biological Psychiatry* 50(9): 677–84; J. K. Rilling, A. L. Glenn. M. R. Jairam, et al. (2007), "Neural correlates of social cooperation and non-cooperation as a function of psychopathy," *Biological Psychiatry* 61(11): 1260–71.

page 52   **accounts for the sociopath's inability to understand emotions:** K. A. Kiehl, "Without Morals," in *Moral Psychology, Volume 3: The Neuroscience of Morality: Emotion, Brain Disorders, and Development,* ed. Walter Sinnott-Armstrong (Cambridge, MA: Massachusetts Institute of Technology Press, 2008).

page 52   **failure to attach emotionally to other people:** Stout, *The Sociopath Next Door.*

page 52   **rooted in neurological lovelessness:** Whether this difference in the brain is random (a result of genetic drift or some other neutral process of evolution), or perhaps bestowed by some naturally selected survival function on groups of our primeval ancestors, is subject to debate; however, since the human species no longer lives in the wild, this survival function, if it ever existed, has almost certainly been obviated, just as the desire to overeat has long outlasted the feast-or-famine conditions of our ancient forebears and now merely plagues us.

page 52   **magnetic resonance imaging studies in the United States, England, and Germany:** American and British: A. P. Jones, K. R. Laurens, C. M. Herba, et al. (2009), "Amygdala hypoactivity to fearful faces in boys with conduct problems and callous-unemotional traits," *American Journal of Psychiatry* 166(1): 95–102; M. J. Kruesi, M. F. Casanova, G. Mannheim, and A. Johnson-Bilder (2004), "Reduced temporal lobe volume in early onset conduct disorder," *Psychiatry Research* 132(1): 1–11; A. A. Marsh, E. C. Finger, D. G. V. Mitchell, et al. (2008), "Reduced amygdala response to fearful expressions in children and adolescents with callous-unemotional traits and disruptive behavior disorders," *American Journal of Psychiatry* 165(6): 712–20; L. Passamonti, G. Fairchild, I. M. Goodyer, et al. (2010), "Neural abnormalities in early-onset and adolescence-onset conduct disorder," *Archives of General Psychiatry* 67(7): 729–38; A. Raine, L. Lee, Y. Yang, P. Colletti (2010), "Neurodevelopmental marker for limbic maldevelopment in antisocial personality disorder and psychopathy," *British Journal of Psychiatry* 197(3): 186–92; Paul Ekman and Wallace V. Friesen, *Pictures of Facial Affect* (Palo Alto, CA: Consulting Psychologists Press, 1976). German: T. Huebner, T. D. Vloet, I. Marx, et al. (2008), "Morphometric brain abnormalities in boys with conduct disorder," *Journal of the American Academy of Child & Adolescent Psychiatry* 47(5): 540–47.

page 52   **German study, which looked at early-onset conduct disorder in boys:** Huebner et al., "Morphometric brain abnormalities in boys with conduct disorder."

page 53   **British neuroimaging study of girls:** G. Fairchild, C. C. Hagan, N. D. Walsh, et al. (2013), "Brain structure abnormalities in adolescent girls with conduct disorder," *Journal of Child Psychology and Psychiatry* 54(1): 86–95.

Here is an overall review of the neurobiology of psychopathy: M. A. Cummings (2015), "The neurobiology of psychopathy: Recent developments and new directions in research and treatment," *CNS Spectrums* 20(3): 200–206.

page 59   **typically 90 to 120 days:** A. L. Patenaude, "History of the Treatment of and Attitudes Toward Children," in *Handbook of Juvenile Justice: Theory and Practice,* ed. Barbara Sims and Pamela Preston (Boca Raton: CRC Press, 2006), 3–30, especially page 22. On advertised treatments, see E. J. Latessa et al. (2002), "Beyond Correctional Quackery-Professionalism and the Possibility of Effective Treatment," *Federal Probation* 66(2): 43, 44.

page 59   **Research has shown that treatments carried out with groups:** T. J. Dishion, J. McCord, and F. Poulin (1999), "When interventions harm. Peer groups and problem behavior," *American Psychologist* 54(9): 755–64.

page 61   **the Kazdin Method:** Alan E. Kazdin, *The Kazdin Method for Parenting the Defiant Child* (New York: Mariner Books, 2008), 39; A. E. Kazdin (1993), "Treatment of conduct disorder: Progress and directions in psychotherapy research," *Development and Psychopathology* 5(1–2): 277–310.

page 64   **the most effective therapeutic approach:** Scott W. Henggeler, Sonja K. Schoenwald, Charles M. Borduin, et al. *Multisystemic Treatment for Antisocial Behavior in Youth* (New York: Guilford Press, 2000).

page 65   **Kazdin has remarked that:** Kazdin, *Kazdin Method,* 39.

THREE. HUMAN EVIL AT WORK: SOCIOPATHIC COWORKERS, BOSSES, AND PROFESSIONALS

page 86   **primatologist Frans de Waal states:** Frans de Waal, *Primates and Philosophers: How Morality Evolved* (Princeton, NJ: Princeton University Press, 2006), 44.

page 86   **Ethologist Marc Bekoff:** Marc Bekoff and Jessica Pierce, *Wild Justice: The Moral Lives of Animals* (Chicago: University of Chicago Press, 2010); the quote is on page 56.

page 88   **When it passes near us:** Cf. Mary Oliver, "Poem for the Anniversary," *Dream Work* (New York: Atlantic Monthly Press, 1986).

page 114   **Bradley Schwartz:** Story from R. Reisner, "Bradley Schwartz: Short-sighted ophthalmologist," *Forensic Files Now*, May 17, 2018; A. H. Rotstein, "Prosecutor: Obsession, rage fueled doctor's murder-for-hire," *Arizona Daily Sun*, March 7, 2006; K. Smith, "Former Tucson doctor doing time for murder sues Ariz. prison system," *Arizona Daily Star*, March 25, 2009; and K. Smith, "The woman at the eye of the storm," *Arizona Daily Star*, February 26, 2006.

page 115   **wrote a book about it:** A. J. Flick, *Toxic Rage: A Tale of Murder in Tucson* (Evergreen, CO: Wildblue Press, 2018).

FOUR. THE SOCIOPATH IN COURT: FIGHTING FOR CHILD CUSTODY

page 133   **it is arguable that two involved parents are better than one:** Robert E. Emery, *Marriage, Divorce, and Children's Adjustment: Developmental Clinical Psychology and Psychiatry*, 2nd ed. (Thousand Oaks, CA: Sage, 1999).

page 137   **Psychologist Adrian Raine:** A. Raine (2009), "Psychopathy and instrumental aggression: Evolutionary, neurobiological, and legal perspectives," *International Journal of Law and Psychiatry* 32(4): 257.

page 140   **In 2002, Peter Jaffe:** Peter Jaffe, Nancy Lemon, and Samantha Poisson, *Child Custody & Domestic Violence: A Call for Safety and Accountability* (Thousand Oaks, CA: Sage Knowledge, 2003); the quote is on page 21.

page 141   **a review of twenty-four separate studies:** Penelope Trickett and Cynthia Schellenbach, eds., *Violence Against Children in the Family and the Community* (Washington, DC: American Psychological Association, 1998).

page 141   **"one may conclude that":** G. Margolin, "Effects of Domestic Violence on Children," in *Violence Against Children in the Family and the Community*, ed. Trickett and Schellenbach, 57–101.

page 142 **In a 1998 report:** A. Appel and G. Holden (1998), "The co-occurrence of spouse and physical child abuse: A review and appraisal," *Journal of Family Psychology* 12(4): 578–99.

page 142 **"Abuse of children by a batterer":** Barbara J. Hart, *Barbara J. Hart's Collected Writings,* Minnesota Center Against Violence and Abuse, p. 12.

page 143 **National Council of Juvenile and Family Court Judges:** S. Schecter and J. L. Edleson, "Effective Intervention in Domestic Violence & Child Maltreatment Cases: Guidelines for Policy and Practice Recommendations from the National Council of Juvenile and Family Court Judges Family Violence Department," National Council of Juvenile and Family Court Judges, June 1999, p. 2, https://www.rcdvcpc.org/media/greenbook/executive_summary.pdf.

page 145 **Attorney Rebecca Kiessling:** Quoted in "A Question of Proof," *The Economist,* July 19, 2014.

FIVE. THE ICIEST OF ALL: ASSAULTIVE AND
HOMICIDAL SOCIOPATHS

page 166 **"just because he could":** M. Davey, "Suspect in 10 Kansas Murders Lived an Intensely Ordinary Life," *New York Times,* March 6, 2005.

page 175 **In 2002, the *Journal of Abnormal Psychology*:** M. Woodworth and S. Porter (2002), "In cold blood: Characteristics of criminal homicides as a function of psychopathy," *Journal of Abnormal Psychology* 111(3): 436–45.

page 176 **A review of forty-five years of research:** D. J. Devine, L. D. Clayton, B. B. Dunford, et al. (2000), "Jury decision making: 45 years of empirical research on deliberating groups," *Psychology Public Policy and Law* 7(3): 622–727.

page 177 **"Viewing the autopsy photos":** Greg Beratlis, Tom Marino, Mike Belmessieri, et al., *We, the Jury: Deciding the Scott Peterson Case* (Beverly Hills, CA: Phoenix Books, 2006); the quote is on pages 54–55.

page 179 **University of San Francisco professor David Vann:** David Vann,

Last Day on Earth: A Portrait of the NIU School Shooter (Athens, GA: University of Georgia Press, 2013).

page 180 **"The degree of self-destruction":** Interview with David Vann, aired on CNN, February 14, 2009, http://edition.cnn.com/TRANSCRIPTS /0902/14/cnr.07.html.

page 183 **Conducted in the Netherlands:** M. van Geel, P. Vedder, and J. Tanilon, "Relationship between peer victimization, bullying, and suicide in children and adolescents: A meta-analysis," March 10, 2014, JAMA Network, https://jamanetwork.com/journals/jamapediatrics/fullarticle/ 1840250.

page 184 **"I don't want the kids to be more resilient":** Parry Aftab, quoted in Ron Kemp, "They Wore Blue," blog post, https://ronskemp.wordpress .com/tag/baltimore-sun/.

SIX. TRANSCENDING THE SOCIOPATH'S EFFECTS:
TEN KEY GUIDELINES

page 187 **In 1959, a Brown University psychologist:** R. Church (1959), "Emotional reactions of rats to the pain of others," *Journal of Comparative and Physiological Psychology* 52(2): 132–34.

page 188 **a study at McGill University:** I. Ganguli, "Mice show evidence of empathy," *The Scientist*, June 30, 2006.

page 188 **animal behaviorist Frans de Waal:** F. B. M. de Waal (1989), "Food sharing and reciprocal obligations among chimpanzees," *Journal of Human Evolution* 18(5): 433–59.

page 191 **a meta-analysis of twenty studies:** A. A. Marsh and R. J. R. Blair (2008), "Deficits in facial affect recognition among antisocial populations: A meta-analysis," *Neuroscience & Biobehavioral Reviews* 32(3): 454–65; the quote is on page 454.

page 191 **the sociologist Edvard Westermarck:** Edward Westermarck, *The Origin and Development of the Moral Ideas,* vol. 1, 2nd ed. (London: Macmillan, 2008).

page 203 **"Before our next breakfast":** Gavin de Becker, *The Gift of Fear: And*

Other Survival Signals That Protect Us from Violence (New York: Little, Brown, 1997), 185. This book is a good resource for interpreting your anxiety and enhancing your personal safety.

SEVEN. SOCIOPATH OR NARCISSIST?: RECOGNIZING NARCISSISTIC PERSONALITY DISORDER

page 214 **is unwilling to recognize or identify:** Note that it says "unwilling." There is a debate over whether this should be "unable" (it probably should be). This shows how even professionals become frustrated and angry with narcissists.

page 216 **In *The Destructive Narcissistic Pattern*:** Nina W. Brown, *The Destructive Narcissistic Pattern* (Westport, CT: Praeger Publishers, 1998), 121. See also Elaine Hatfield, John C. Cacioppo, and Richard L. Rapson, *Emotional Contagion: Studies in Emotion and Social Interaction* (Paris: Cambridge University Press, 1993).

page 218 **The psychoanalyst Otto Fenichel:** O. Fenichel (1938), "The drive to amass wealth," *Psychoanalytic Quarterly* 7(1): 69–95.

page 221 **Even trained clinicians tend to get angry with narcissists:** G. O. Gabbard, "Transference and Countertransference in Treatment of Narcissistic Patients," in *Disorders of Narcissism: Diagnostic, Clinical, and Empirical Implications,* ed. Elsa F. Ronningstam (Washington, DC: American Psychiatric Press, 1998), 125–46. See also G. L. Lynn and S. Jortner (1976), "The use of countertransference as a way to understand and treat patients," *Journal of Contemporary Psychotherapy* 8(1): 15–18; E. J. Betan and D. Westen, "Countertransference and Personality Pathology: Development and Clinical Application of the Countertransference Questionnaire," in *Handbook of Evidence-Based Psychodynamic Psychotherapy: Bridging the Gap Between Science and Practice,* ed. Raymond A. Levy and J. Stuart Ablon, foreword by G. O. Gabbard (New York: Humana Press, 2010), 179–98.

page 225 **The narcissist feels he is above the law:** See John Murray's classic paper on the "narcissistic triad" (narcissistic entitlement, disappointment and disillusionment at the frustration of narcissistic needs, and narcissistic rage): John Murray (1964), "Narcissism and the ego ideal," *Journal of the American Psychoanalytic Association* 12(3): 477–511.

EIGHT. SOCIOPATHY AT THE INSTITUTIONAL
LEVEL: CORPORATIONS AND GOVERNMENTS

page 234 **Overall, research indicates that:** J. F. Edens, J. L. Skeem, and P. Kennealy, "The Psychopathy Checklist in the Courtroom: Consensus and Controversies," in *Psychological Science in the Courtroom: Consensus and Controversy*, ed. Jennifer L. Skeem, Kevin S. Douglas, and Scott O. Lilienfeld (New York: Guilford Press, 2009), 175–201.

page 234 **the Hare Psychopathy Checklist can be reliably scored:** Robert D. Hare, *Manual for the Revised Psychopathy Checklist*, 2nd ed. (Toronto: Multi-Health Systems, 2003); R. D. Hare and C. S. Neumann, "The PCL-R Assessment of Psychopathy: Development, Structural Properties, and New Directions," in *Handbook of Psychopathy*, ed. Christopher J. Patrick (New York: Guilford Press, 2006), 58–88.

page 235 **"singularly self-interested":** Joel Bakan, *The Corporation: The Pathological Pursuit of Profit and Power* (New York: Free Press, 2005), 56.

page 236 **Bakan states that the corporation:** Ibid., pp. 28, 60.

page 236 **PCBs, which were banned by the EPA in the 1970s:** "Monsanto's Dirty Dozen: Twelve Products that Monsanto Has Brought to Market," Global Research, Centre for Research on Globalization, July 25, 2016, https://www.globalresearch.ca/monsantos-dirty-dozen-twelve-products-that-monsanto-has-brought-to-market/5537809.

page 237 **concern about Roundup's potential impact:** B. S. Hooker, "Rounding up glyphosate," *Focus for Health*, September 5, 2018, https://www.focusforhealth.org/rounding-up-glyphosate/.

page 237 **47,000 overdose deaths:** B. Meier, "Sacklers directed efforts to mislead public about OxyContin, new documents indicate," *New York Times*, January 15, 2019.

page 238 **$634.5 million in fines:** Ibid.

page 238 **"turbocharge" sales of OxyContin:** M. Forsythe and W. Bogdanich, "McKinsey advised Purdue Pharma how to 'turbocharge' opioid sales, lawsuit says," *New York Times,* February 1, 2019.

page 238 **A reassessment of published research on Paxil:** J. Le Noury, J. M. Nardo, D. Healy, et al. (2015), "Restoring Study 329: Efficacy and harms of paroxetine and imipramine in treatment of major depression in adolescence," *British Medical Journal* 351: h4320.

page 238 **Although cigarette smoking among adults in the United States has declined:** "Cigarette smoking remains high among certain groups," Centers for Disease Control and Prevention, Press Release, January 18, 2018, page 2, https://www.cdc.gov/media/releases/2018/p0118-smoking-rates -declining.html.

page 239 **more than seven thousand articles related to smoking and disease:** U.S. Department of Health and Human Services, "The Health Consequences of Smoking—50 Years of Progress: A Report of the Surgeon General," Executive Summary, 2014, p. 5, https://www.surgeongeneral.gov /library/reports/50-years-of-progress/full-report.pdf.

page 239 **Yet internal documents have revealed that:** T. Lewan (1998), "Dark secrets of tobacco company exposed," *Tobacco Control* 7(3): 315–18.

page 239 **the new design would result in 180 fewer deaths:** M. T. Lee and M. D. Ermann, "Pinto 'madness' as a flawed landmark narrative: An organizational and network analysis," *Social Problems* 46(1): 38.

page 240 **"The scandals have arrived":** Bakan, *The Corporation,* p. 42.

page 240 **The famous Stanley Milgram studies on obedience to authority:** S. Milgram, "Behavioral study of obedience," *Journal of Abnormal and Social Psychology* 67(4): 371–78. See also Stanley Milgram, *Obedience to Authority: An Experimental View* (New York: Psychology,1983); and Thomas Blass, ed., *Obedience to Authority: Current Perspectives on the Milgram Paradigm* (Mahwah, NJ: Lawrence Erlbaum Associates, 2000).

page 241 **twenty-six of Milgram's original forty subjects:** Milgram, "Behavioral Study of Obedience."

page 241 **A subsequent study with women:** T. Blass (1999), "The Milgram paradigm after 35 years: Some things we now know about obedience to authority," *Journal of Applied Social Psychology* 29(5): 968.

page 241 **"A substantial proportion of people will do what they are told to do":** S. Milgram (1965), "Some conditions of obedience and disobedience to authority," *Human Relations* 18(1): 57–76.

page 242 **This term was coined by Ervin Staub:** Ervin Staub, *The Roots of Evil: The Origins of Genocide and Other Group Violence* (New York: Cambridge University Press, 1989).

page 242 **"Ordinary people may simply be acting":** G. Adams and D. Balfour, "Human Rights, the Moral Vacuum of Modern Organisations, and Administrative Evil," in *Human Rights and the Moral Responsibilities of Corporate and Public Sector Organisations,* ed. Tom Campbell and Seumas Miller (New York: Springer, 2004), 208.

page 242 **"Because administrative evil is typically masked":** Ibid. See also G. B. Adams, D. L Balfour, and G. E. Reed (2006), "Abu Ghraib, administrative evil, and moral inversion: The value of 'putting cruelty first,'" *Public Administration Review* 66(5): 680–93; and G. Adams and D. Balfour, *Unmasking Administrative Evil* (Armonk, NY: M. E. Sharpe, 2009).

page 244 **even a psychiatrist's diagnosis of him:** M. Stal (2013), "Psychopathology of Joseph Stalin," *Psychology* 4(9): 1–4.

page 245 **may have resulted in more than three million deaths:** P. Heuveline (2015), "The Boundaries of genocide: Quantifying the uncertainty of the death toll during the Pol Pot regime (1975–1979)," *Population Studies* 69(2): 201.

page 246 **"contradicts almost every other serious effort":** I. Johnson, "Who Killed More: Hitler, Stalin, or Mao?," *New York Review of Books*, February 5, 2018.

NINE. THE NATURE OF GOOD: COMPASSION,
FORGIVENESS, AND FREEDOM

page 251 **In 1971, Gerald Mayo:** *United States ex rel. Gerald Mayo v. Satan and His Staff,* 54 F.R.D. 282 (1971).

page 252 **psychiatric anthropologist Jane M. Murphy describes the Inuit concept:** J. Murphy (1976), "Psychiatric labeling in cross-cultural perspective: Similar kinds of disturbed behavior appear to be labeled abnormal in diverse cultures," *Science* 191(4231): 1019–28.

page 253 **Sebastian Junger notes that our modern society:** Sebastian Junger, *Tribe: On Homecoming and Belonging* (New York: Twelve, 2016), 28.

page 254 **Healthy Workplace Bill:** D. C. Yamada (2010), "Workplace bullying and American employment law: A ten-year progress report and assessment," *Comparative Labor Law & Policy Journal* 32(1): 251. Available at SSRN: http://ssrn.com/abstract=1908465. Also see the Healthy Workplace Bill website, where you can volunteer to help stop workplace bullying: https://healthyworkplacebill.org/.

page 260 **"blue baby syndrome":** Joyce Baldwin, *To Heal the Heart of a Child: Helen Taussig, M.D.* (New York: Walker, 1992); and Vivien T. Thomas, *Partners of the Heart: Vivien Thomas and His Work with Alfred Blalock: An Autobiography* (Philadelphia: University of Pennsylvania Press, 1998).

page 260 *positive psychology:* See Martin E. P. Seligman, *Authentic Happiness: Using the New Positive Psychology to Realize Your Potential for Lasting Fulfillment* (New York: Free Press, 2002); Martin E. P. Seligman, *Flourish: A Visionary New Understanding of Happiness and Well-Being* (New York: Free Press, 2011); Martin E. P. Seligman, *The Hope Circuit: A Psychologist's Journey from Helplessness to Optimism* (New York: PublicAffairs Books, 2018); and Christopher Peterson, *Pursuing the Good Life: 100 Reflections on Positive Psychology* (New York: Oxford University Press, 2012).

ACKNOWLEDGMENTS

In September 2018, just as I finished writing this book, I had a small stroke. I might not even have noticed it if it hadn't caused me to lose consciousness for a moment and to fall hard, onto my right side, on the asphalt of a nearly empty parking lot. I am amnesic for the fall and for much that happened immediately afterward, but I'm told that five strangers gathered and made the decision to call trauma services for me. I never met any of them before, during, or after my fall, but would give much to know their identities so that I could thank them deeply for, in all probability, saving my life.

The black eye faded, and I recovered my original face, my speaking voice, all cognitive capacity, and the nerve to walk, though I still have vertigo from time to time. At the rehabilitation center, I was most fortunate to meet Dr. Jonathan Perry, a fellow psychologist, who assured me that after some months had passed, we would have coffee together and express our amazement at how horrible this time had been and how miraculous that it was all over, no more vertigo or fatigue. It would all be a thing of the past. His dignity, and the courage he had to tell me calmly about having recovered from a similar problem himself, got me through that time, and I very much look forward to having coffee together one fine day. The five strangers saved my life the first time, and in his way, Dr. Perry saved my life (with hope) a second time. I needed it.

Enter Linda Carbone, the seventh hero, to save the book. Linda is an editor and author. (She and her husband, Ed Decker, wrote a moving book called *A Little Pregnant,* which I highly recommend.) After a book has been written, there are many things to do before it can go into production. In the past, I had happily taken care of these things myself, but this time I could not. Chapters had to be placed in their final order and information filled in. Endnotes had to be arranged properly and, in some cases, retrieved. Someone needed to communicate with the publisher regarding the layout and general appearance of the book. It is very difficult for anyone to step in and take these tasks over for an author (authors are highly possessive people), but Linda did so gracefully and skillfully and (for me) almost painlessly. She is a very special person, and I am endlessly grateful to her. Thank you, Linda.

I thank my very fine editorial director, Diana Baroni, for her vision and her patience, and my other editors—Charlie Conrad, Leah Miller, and Amanda Patten—for their invaluable help, some of them during a tumultuous time in their own lives. For her help in finalizing the manuscript, and in making it what it is, I would like to express my great appreciation to Michele Eniclerico, who was able to maintain a clear and coherent conception of the book through all its transitions.

I wish to thank people from my personal life as well: my beloved and brilliant daughter, Amanda Kielley, and her handsome and poetic husband, Nick Delahaye, both of whom have an exquisite eye and can be counted upon to see the things that count; my brother and lifelong friend, Steve Stout, and his perfect-pick fiancée, Christine Bessett (who will be his wife by the time anyone reads this), and Howard Kielley, who shared his house with me and lent a dizzy me his watchful eye—I bless you for your kindness.

I would like to express my gratitude to all the readers who wrote to me after reading *The Sociopath Next Door*. If I could have included every single letter, I would have. The stories I used have been changed in the interest of anonymity, but if it had been possible, I would have written the real names in large letters, in the interest of revealing courage and assigning credit.

Last but never least, I thank my incredibly gifted literary agent, Susan Lee Cohen. Susan is all an agent should be and more, and all a human being should be in a perfect world. As I tell her (but not frequently enough), she is my miracle worker. She does not really know what I mean, but I know that it is her skill and grace that made it possible for me to achieve my childhood dream of being a writer. Let me say it again: thank you, Susan.

INDEX

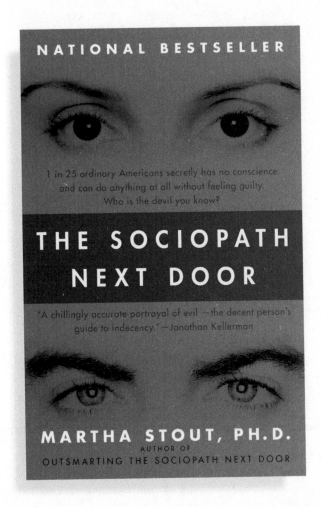